DSL

DOWN | SET | LEAD!

DOWN | SET | LEAD!

The Ultimate Playbook for Building
Your Leadership Confidence

ROD BOURN

ISBN: 979-8-9871475-0-4 (paperback)
ISBN: 979-8-9871475-1-1 (ebook)

Book design by M.V. McLaughlin

Print in the United States

DOWN, SET, LEAD

DOWN, SET, LEAD!

The Ultimate Playbook for Building Your Leadership Confidence

Down – in the dirt, sift out what you have

Set – the stance and pick the right posture

Lead – the group, facilitate the opportunities

Chapters

Determine – your current culture (are they Vets? Young? Winners? Beaten dogs? A mix?)

Own – the responsibility (lead from out front and communicate)

Weigh – the costs (of keeping vs. cutting the disengaged)

Negotiate – your final roster (top young talent, projects, free agents, and vets)

Sell – the vision

Enlist – team members in their role

Train – on the basics as well as to their interests

Listen – to what they want (their passions)

Empower – them to do their job and more

Advocate – for your team members

Develop – them through your mentorship, and into becoming mentors themselves

FORWARD

Hi, and kudos for bothering to read this page. I mean, who actually reads Forwards?? You must be in an airport shop waiting for a delayed flight—my condolences.

The good news is you're *this close* to reading some entertaining stories and getting some interesting and maybe even powerful leadership perspectives tied to movie quotes (movie quotes!), all with a football motif. I've even thrown in some quick exercises for you to try so you can gauge how you're doing as a leader. And maybe you will get an idea or two on how to rejuvenate yourself and/or your team. All in 100 easy pages.

So go ahead and flip through for a moment. Chuckle at something or give a thoughtful sounding "hmm" loud enough for the person near you buying a t-shirt for their kid back home to hear. And if you want a challenge, look at them, hold this book up and say, "this looks like a good read!" While I can't promise you any royalties, your karma points will certainly rise and you'll have my gracious thanks.

Otherwise, just carefully place this back (don't dog-ear the corner—no one buys dog-eared paperbacks!) and move on down to join your new friend in the t-shirt section. And have a safe flight!

Best,
Rod

Editor's Note:

Rod is modest. This book is a must-read for organizational leaders and want-to-be leaders. The guidance and insight will make you a better leader. No kidding!

— LEE CRUMBAUGH,
SMP, FORREST CONSULTING

AUTHOR'S NOTES

My background is in Human Resources; I spent nearly two decades in the field in a variety of industries as I rose from a management trainee at a famous clothing manufacturer to overseeing a large HR office in a huge distribution facility for a well-known drug store chain. As all HR professionals can tell you, truth is far stranger than fiction, just ask any of us to share some the stories of the investigations we've had to run on people doing stupid things at work. It's from those years and experiences I learned so much about what works and what doesn't regarding leadership.

I've laid this book out with a couple of unique items. At the beginning of each chapter you will see a movie quote because 1) movie quotes are fun, and 2) hopefully they help you focus on the chapter's topic.

At the end of each chapter I have added a "Go to the Replay Booth" page to capture the key points of that section.

The book is a chronology of leadership; you have to accomplish "Determine your current culture" before you can accomplish "Own the responsibility," "Weigh the costs," "Negotiate your final roster," and so on.

Throughout the book are Contributor Addendums, thoughts I've collected from former players, coaches and executives who have added their thoughts on one of the book's topics (specifically Own, Negotiate, Empower, and Listen). I feel blessed to have connected with these gentlemen and appreciate their special takes. Towards the end of the book each Contributor has a page dedicated to them and how to get in touch with them. I highly recommend you do reach out to them, and partner as you can. They are all great guys!

I've intentionally included some white space throughout the book for you to make notes, and encourage you to do so. That's because if you read something you have a decent chance of retaining it. But if you read and write something down, you have a much greater chance of remembering points important to you. The "Go to the Replay Booth" pages may be good for you to also put your key take-aways. So get out that clipboard and get makin' with those X's and O's (and those other 24 letters, too).

OPENING

(Cue ESPN theme music and crowd noise in the background)

The team breaks from the huddle as Johnson slaps his hands and tightens his chin strap. He looks over the defense as he readies to take the snap from Kartowski. He notices Ridel sneaking up from his linebacker position while Pi'atu shuffles from leaning over the guard to the B gap. Jones runs as expected from left to right behind him, stopping to the right of Handy and looking back at Johnson.

Johnson steps back and audibles. The line shifts and the fullback McCarney comes forward to stand beside him. Quickly Johnson steps back in under Kartowski and yells, "HIKE!"

Suddenly 22 bodies move in a choreography of memorized steps, making adjustments on the fly as they try to meet their goal. Individual battles, two-on-ones, improvising as familiarity allows; it all happens at the highest level every weekend in the fall and winter.

Such is life on the gridiron, where individuals and teams are challenged by schemes devised by brilliant (and sometimes not-so-brilliant) adversaries standing across the field, headset on and clipboard in hand.

Similar is life Mondays through Fridays (and weekends, too) in every organization in America and across the world. Granted there aren't 80,000 screaming fans (or even 40,000 mildly interested ones—sorry Commanders fans) cheering, jeering, and everything in between while proposals are being written and P&L statements verified. But there are hundreds, thousands, and millions of dollars being proposed, processed, and posted every hour. And you, as a decision maker, need to lead your team to be as effective and prosperous as possible, all while maintaining a positive culture and keeping the boss happy. It's near impossible—look at the NFL—just one perfect season *ever*. But there have been many extremely good, close-to-perfect teams who've become the stuff of legends. So good that they have earned nicknames (e.g., The Legion of Doom, The Greatest Show on Turf, The Steel Curtain, and The Purple People Eaters). And while no one could tell you the name of any team in any business organization, many deserve a nickname, and yours could too.

It begins with a commitment, the willingness to take time out of every day to take a bird's eye view of your team's situation and, whenever necessary, call an audible to make adjustments. Depending on your natural skill set this may be easy or not, but it's doable by anyone who puts their mind to it. Just as a quarterback calls "down, set, hike," every manager has the opportunity to reflect on how they get down, set themselves, and then lead into the issues of the day, and pull out a profitable and successful outcome that involves all the talents of the team. Or, in other words, "Down, Set, Lead"!

PART ONE

DOWN

Sifting Through the Dirt to See What You Have

DETERMINE

The D in "DOWN" stands for Determining your Culture and Skills.

"You're a disease. And I'm the cure."

— SYLVESTER STALLONE
AS MARION COBRETTI, *COBRA (1986)*

Congratulations, you have been selected to lead a team! Or maybe you've been leading a team and you're just looking for some fresh ideas. Perhaps you feel like you're stuck in a rut. Whatever, you CAN learn how to get from where you are to where you want to be.

Sly's quote above is a heady declaration that he's gonna right the situation, and that's what employees want to hear—someone's gonna make things better! The first step in leading is determining *What Exactly You Are Getting Into?* It sounds like a daunting task, but it is actually easy if you do it in steps. Just like the riddle goes: How do you eat an elephant? One bite at a time. That's the same idea here. You take this step by step, bite by bite, play by play.

Dynasties ain't built overnight, after all. The Green Bay Packer powerhouses of the 60s took years to build. The Pittsburgh Steelers of the 70s, San Francisco 49ers of the 80s, Dallas Cowboys of the 90s, and

New England Patriots until recently, all started with small steps that got larger as they developed success.

Success depends on your resources. They need to be complementary. You could have the two best quarterbacks in the league on your team, but you only need superstar QB (and a decent backup). And if you don't have a line to protect them, receivers to throw to, and a defense to stop the other team, you're pretty much spinning your wheels. And if you're spinning your wheels in football, work, or life, you're going to lose. And if you don't do anything about it, you will continue to lose. And then you become that lovable loser, or the team no player will join if they want to win. You may even become a pariah and find it's become harder to grow sales or attract clients because of your reputation. And it all rests on the resources you have, how well they reinforce one other, and how well they fit into your goal.

Like most anything else, good leadership starts at the beginning, with your current situation, your current roster, and your current resources.

Let's take the easier assumption first: You are entering a new employment situation and will be managing a team of employees. Hopefully you did your recon during the interview process, learning about the personality and reputation of the group. What you need is specific, honest intel. Did you talk culture with those who interviewed you? Who are you taking over for, and more importantly why? What was their style and how did it work with the team they were leading? If you didn't ask questions like these, and you're still in the hiring process, you can still go back and ask these important questions. As an HR professional, my attention would be piqued if an applicant asked questions like these.

As you are listening to people talk about your area, do you see any themes emerge? How does the team break down in terms of experience and performance? If you are a visual learner, literally sketch it out on a sheet of paper so you can better view the situation (think of this as basic analytics).

Ed Catmull, the founder of KickStart, basically said the same when he commented, "Getting the team right is the precursor to getting the ideas right."

If you can, talk with the outgoing manager. It's good to know why they are leaving; invite them out for a coffee or adult beverage so you can get their take on what's going on in the area. (You might get more information if it is over an adult beverage or two, just be careful not to let your tongue get too loose!) Or, if you can't meet in person, there is always Zoom.

On the other hand, even if you've been leading a group for a while, reviewing your line up is something best done with a trusted point of view from outside your area. Most people have difficulty getting a clear picture of the situation they are in.

You may have heard the tale of the frog, who when put in a pot of hot water immediately jumped out. But when put in a pot of warm water he stayed, and he continued to stay even as the temperature gradually rose. He eventually became soup, because he didn't realize the slow and dangerous change in his environment.

My point: Don't become Frog Soup because of your pride in staying your course. No one likes Frog Soup. Eventually Frog Soup gets a bad reputation and/or thrown out.

You need to ask yourself: "What exactly is our team's/department's/division's culture and why?" There are tons of great books on this. You can YouTube it, but the definition of culture essentially comes down to this: *The values and beliefs that create the environment of your office space.*

Ok, sounds kinda esoteric, I know. In layman's terms it's basically *how does it feel when someone walks in your area?* Or if they monitor the team on Slack or visit one of the team's Zoom meetings?

You can get a great picture of your situation in four steps:

STEP 1: Picture It

Start with yourself. Be honest, list three things YOU feel when you walk in to your (office) area.

1. _____

2. _____

3. _____

Now, just as importantly ask the same of people you trust and who spend some time in your area (clients, partners, but NOT the employees themselves, you want the opinions of someone from outside your area).

Now you should ask yourself how do you <u>want</u> your office to feel to someone (clients, workers, your boss) who walks in? List the top few things you want people to feel.

1. _____

2. _____

3. _____

So you can guess what's next—compare and contrast. What are people (including you) feeling when they walk in versus what you want them to feel. How big is the gap: Slight? Modest? Huge?

Before really delving in, let's throw some extra clarity on this by looking at places you think have great cultures. Think about the "feel" of your favorite restaurant. Now your favorite bar. Now your favorite store. That "feel" you get is because of the culture, which either intentionally or unintentionally comes from the leader(s) of that business. It also comes from the physical design, level of cleanliness, efficiency and order of a place. If it's something you really like, it's probably intentional, although it could just be an extension of that leader's/owner's personality (which is not at all uncommon). I'll give an example below from my personal take:

PLACE	THE FEEL IT HAS	I LIKE IT BECAUSE	THINGS I'D LIKE TO REPLICATE FROM IT
Restaurant – Hard Yacht Cafe	Busy, open, fun, beachy	There's a fun beachy buzz; tables aren't on top of each other; staff is VERY friendly; food is good quality and not expensive	Friendly, fun vibe, good but not over-the-top energy
Bar – Poole's Island	Spacious, well lit, family oriented, clean	Extensive beer menu with descriptions, you can pour your own flights. Owners and staff knowledgeable and talk to you, glad to see you	Variety, I can pour as much or little as I what (not limited as I am in other bars), explanations of offerings, cheeriness
Store – Bass Pro Shop	Huge, lots of great design to their displays; some actually interactive.	I can get lost and not mind because it feels like I'm exploring	Experiences to interact with and sense of exploring
Stadium – Pittsburgh's PNC Park	Intimate, classic	Really well designed/positioned. Sight lines are great	Totally intentional in design, celebrates the city's past and showcases the best skyline in America

Now you try it:

PLACE	THE FEEL IT HAS	I LIKE IT BECAUSE	THINGS I'D LIKE TO REPLICATE FROM IT
Restaurant			
Bar			
Store			
Stadium			
Other place you frequent / love			
Other place you frequent / love			

The key to this is being intentional. In fact, the key to **all** of this is to BE INTENTIONAL. There are some places where the leader has such a big personality that everything inside the walls of the building and out reflect that person. Think of Jerry Jones of the Dallas Cowboys, probably the most well-known NFL owner. Jerry is about BIG, his personality is big, and he's one of the most media covered owners in all of sports. Now you can argue whether his impact is good or bad for the final results (when was the last time Dallas was in the Super Bowl?), but everyone recognizes the brand and the 'boys are one of the most popular *sports* teams in the nation, not just in football. So if you're NOT measuring recent Super Bowl wins he's pretty dang successful (that "dang" was intentional, just trying to get a little Texas on y'all). The logo is known, the players are known, and the money flows in.

But you need to know what it is that YOU want people to feel when they work directly in <u>and</u> with your area. So let's take the key words that jump out at you in the grid above (ones you've mentioned more than once, and then the next 3 to 5 that mean the most to you) and list them out. For me it'd be:

- Spacious / open
- Interactive
- Friendly

For you it'd be:

- _____
- _____
- _____

So, from that list you've generated, how do you create that atmosphere?

If you're intentional about it, it'll be far easier to create. When you look at the **New Leader Onboarding Session** in the back of the book, you'll find a method for clearly establishing your culture from Day 1, to essentially have your first locker room talk focus on the most important thing moving forward—your vision for how you're all going to achieve greater success! From that opening day statement you can send a clear message: this is what we're aiming for, this is how we're doing it, and this is why we are doing it. You don't have to give a detailed lecture; in fact if you do you're missing the entire point of this book. Dynasties aren't built overnight, Rome wasn't built in a day, and it took a whopping 738 days for Bill Belichick to win a Super Bowl from the day he started at New England. (And while he can lay claim to being arguably the greatest professional head coach of all time, at the beginning of the 2022 season he is just 70-79 overall without Brady and 29-58 against teams with a .500 winning percentage or better. Just sayin', but more on that later.)

If you aren't coming in brand new, you can still use the Onboarding Session outline and just focus it around wanting to be more intentional about correcting the course. It'll probably be harder to do, but it will serve as an official notice that you are serious about trying to make improvements, and that starts with communicating better.

STEP 2: Run a Gap Analysis with a Decision Tree

So now that you have some clear idea about what you have and can compare it to what you want, you can take a stab at what's called a Gap Analysis. This will allow you to essentially look at the difference between what you have and what you want so you can work on closing the difference or "gap." Look up Lucidchart, they offer a fine overview on this.

If you want to know which gap/shortcoming to tackle first, ask yourself this: In which area would an impact bring the biggest payback? Think "lowest hanging fruit" here. Once you have that, use an Action Plan and a Decision Tree to make sure you're taking the right path. Again, I'd really encourage you to use the assistance of an outside, trusted advisor, such as the training director in your HR department, if your company has one. The most highly regarded manager in the company will do fine if she has good high-level organizational skills. Or get an outside consultant who has worked in your industry. It can be invaluable to get a pair of outside eyes on an internal problem, someone who isn't involved with the emotions that come with a workplace.

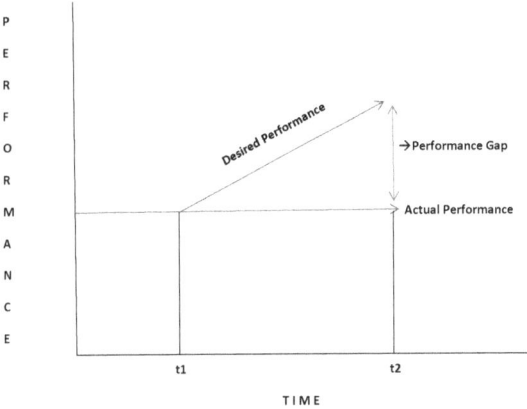

TIME

STEP 3: Your Team SWOTs Itself

As a refresher, SWOT stands for Strengths (internal pluses), Weaknesses (internal minuses), Opportunities (external pluses) and Threats (external minuses). This is a great tool because it focuses in from a variety of angles and can help uncover blind spots you (collectively) may have, such as often responding immediately with an emotional retort.

In a SWOT analysis you have participants develop a list of items under each of the four areas without criticism. You could also/instead do a SOAR analysis; it's arguably a more positive, forward thinking model that focuses on potential. In SOAR you keep the Strengths and Opportunities, but instead use the A for Aspirations of a perfect future, and the R for measureable Results. But I would argue that you miss out on blind sorts if you don't identify and address the Weaknesses and Threats. You can always add in the Aspirations and Results later.

Having a trusted neutral facilitator lead a SWOT analysis of your team by your team (with you <u>not</u> in the room!) may be very useful in getting a read on where your employees' thoughts are on their own pluses and minuses.

One important note should be made before moving forward—this process will only be successful if there's an honest level of trust among your employees. All employees want their organization to be a good one, but if they don't trust their leader(s), they won't risk their positions to offer solid suggestions that could later come back to haunt them. So if you honestly feel there's a pronounced lack of trust, DON'T do the SWOT with employees. All you will get is garble.

Whether that trust is there so your team can SWOT itself, or not, you can then get...

STEP 4: Outsiders SWOT Your Team

Get outsiders' opinions, specifically those of well-reputed, longer term managers familiar with your team. This could be a customer(s), client(s), vendor(s), or counterpart(s) from inside or outside the organization.

Some good questions you could ask include:

- What's my area's reputation? Why? Can you give me examples supporting that?
- Who are my stars? Why?
- Who are my weak links? Why?
- What are the things we do best and worst? Can you give me examples?

From this conversation other questions will probably crop up. Ask them. The more feedback you can get the better. The feedback may not be 100% what's actually happening, but it's the perception of what's going on. Perception is reality!

Ultimately you can (re)create your area's strategic plan that plays to the Strengths and Opportunities while addressing or mitigating the Weaknesses and Threats!

All of this reflection feeds well into building your area's strategic plan, which we will discuss in the chapter SELL.

Key Chapter Points
(a.k.a. – Going to the Replay Booth)

1. Ask about culture during your interview

2. Ask those in the know for details about your new area's reputation

3. Insist on doing a New Leader Onboarding Session as your first act, or a Reset Onboarding session if you've been there a while but want to start intentionally changing the culture

— 2 —

OWN

The O in "DOWN" stands for Own as in Owning the Responsibility

Bluto: Over? Did you say "over"? Nothing is over until we decide it is! Was it over when the Germans bombed Pearl Harbor? Hell no!

Otter: [to Boon] Germans?

Boon: Forget it, he's rolling.

Bluto: And it ain't over now. 'Cause when the goin' gets tough...The tough get goin'! Who's with me? Let's goooooooo!

– JOHN BELUCHI'S BLUTO IN *ANIMAL HOUSE*,
WHO WENT ON TO LEAD ONE OF THE MOST
MEMORABLE RETALIATIONS AGAINST
"DA MAN" IN MOVIE HISTORY.

One of the things I've come to notice in studying organizations is the role leadership plays, specifically how the impact of strong leadership, mild leadership, and inept leadership lead to different outcomes in culture.

The quote above is maybe the most loved and re-quoted lines for many guys, because not only is it ridiculous, but because John goes rushing out of the room ready to lead the charge.

Imagine your organizational chart for a moment. At the very top is the general manager or CEO or COO. Now imagine if she were gone. All the people that report to her would then be at a bit of a loss. If the board of directors decided not to fill that position, there would be a leadership vacuum and inevitably some of those direct reports would most likely vie for the ultimate leadership of the organization, even if it were in an informal/unofficial capacity. This is due to two reasons:

1. Someone **has to** lead the organization. Even when there is no clear leader, someone is going to try to lead from behind scenes, and...

2. If a person with unethical intentions is leading the group from an unofficial position, they are in a glorious position. They can exercise lots of power while not constrained by the responsibility that goes with the "official" head position. That can be a scary proposition because power tends to corrupt, especially if the person wielding it doesn't have to be held accountable.

If you are going to be a truly effective leader, you have to act like one. You have to let people know that you recognize that you are the one that everyone is looking to, and that you understand that you are the one responsible for creating the culture for the organization, even if we are just talking about a department in a division in a corporation. If you want proof, just look for organizations where there are pockets of joy in a marsh of distress, or vice versa.

Of course, acting like the leader in itself is not enough. Being an effective leader also involves earning the respect of those you lead as well as proving yourself.

One of my favorite football leadership stories is about former Indianapolis quarterback Peyton Manning, the very first time he came out on the field as a freshman for Tennessee against Florida after injuries to Todd Helton and Jerry Colquitt took out his more senior counterparts. As Manning ran onto the field he recalled the words his dad Archie had given him a few days earlier: "Even though you're a freshman, take charge of the huddle."[1]

So looking to charge up his teammates, the young Manning attempted to give some words to rally the guys in the huddle. After a sentence or two he was interrupted.

"Shut the ^(#$* up and call the %$^%*ing play," said tackle Jason Layman, three years Manning's senior. So call the play is what Manning did.

Peyton was obviously willing to take the mantel, but he had not yet earned the right to have it, and his performance showed—he and the Vols ultimately lost. But over time his performance in words and deeds took root, both in college and in the pros. And that is sometimes the unfortunate truth in business, the proverbial girl or boy being sent to do a woman's or man's job (or at least a task they probably not quite ready for—a difficult "baptism by fire").

You may have seen or even been involved personally in a similar situation. I have two clear memories myself.

Once very early in my career (I was a 23-year-old Equal Employment Opportunity coordinator in the HR department), the Director of Operations sent me from corporate to a sewing facility to announce to the 200+ employees that their workplace was being closed. A difficult task even for an experienced HR professional!

The other instance came a few years later when I was a fresh HR Manager. I was instructed over the phone by the general manager of the building (Jerry) to fire my boss (Mac, Director of Admin) while Jerry was out of the state on an overnight trip. Now that was an assignment I certainly did not want!

As you can imagine, neither situation went as smoothly as it could and should have gone. The sewing plant became a hive full of questions and anger, workers who had in some cases spent decades at the building wanted answers. I had packets to hand out, and along with the plant manager could handle most of their questions, but they wanted to hear from top leadership why it was happening. And as for the firing, my boss took it relatively well; I think in fact he may had been expecting it, although not from me.

In those two situations had the big bosses been doing their job—taking the lead on the "dirty work", things may have gone better. Years later I realized that having been put in those positions actually helped me become a stronger professional, but at the time it was like asking a rookie with a clipboard to go in and make a successful 4th quarter drive in a big game. I knew what I was supposed to do, but I certainly wasn't the best person for the task.

Rorke Denver, former All-American athlete and 13-year Navy SEAL, said that the best leadership lesson he learned in military training was simple: "Calm is contagious, but so are chaos and panic." And so too is optimism.

Dallas Cowboys Hall of Fame coach Tom Landry put it this way: "Leadership is a matter of having people look at you and gain confidence. If you're in control, they're in control."

It is important to remember that people want to see their managers lead from the front, give clear direction, and jump in to assist, especially when things seem to get overwhelming. To not do so is to undermine the leader's own credibility.

Going beyond tackling the tasks at hand, a truly effective leader works magic with these three words:

Leaders Facilitate Opportunity

Reflect on that a minute.

What does it mean to facilitate opportunity? To me it means talking one-on-one with your employees to reflect on what it is they are trying to achieve (start with what's on their annual review as a goal for the year), asking <u>what</u> <u>specific</u> <u>obstacles</u> *they* think are in their way, and helping the employee get over, around or through it. This doesn't at all mean for you to do their job, but instead to understand what (in their eyes) they are facing and help them figure out how to clear the path. It may mean finding or shifting funds, or talking to a stubborn gatekeeper, or facilitating an introduction.

In discussing ways around obstacles you are not only 1) helping an employee get a job done, but 2) developing greater trust with that employee. Again, you aren't doing their task for them, but rather are assisting in getting the "clutter" out of their way so they can accomplish it and move on to the next job. This 3) builds the employee's confidence, making them stronger and more engaged.

Have you ever started working for a new company and heard co-workers talk about "the good ol' days"? The next time you do, ask them why they were so good, what changed, and how it could be recaptured. You might hear a tale of good people gone, new conditions or restrictions, or less money and/or attention given to the employees.

While that may be the case, I want to point you to the list in the appendix showing what employees really want, and understand that you can still create an oasis in that desert.

Owning the Responsibility makes me think of President Truman's famous "The Buck Stops Here" line, derived from the slang expression "pass the buck," which means passing the responsibility on to someone else (supposedly from passing a buck knife from player to player around the poker table).

You see this from time to time in football locker room or post-game interviews. One of the more fun things to watch is a coach's reaction after the game. Some take responsibility, like Jim Mora, then the Indianapolis Colt's coach, in his infamous "Playoffs?!" rant after his team's dismal loss to the 49er's. So did Arizona Cardinal's coach Dennis Green in his "But they are who we thought they were! And we let 'em off the hook!" tirade after the Chicago Bears made up a 20-point half-time deficit to beat the Cardinals. (Both of these blow-ups can be found on YouTube: Fun viewing!)

Then there are times when the coach realizes they stole a game and are darn lucky that their team literally got a lucky bounce, the opposition didn't make a crucial play, or the refs missed something to his team's benefit. They have a smile on their face like the cat who ate the canary.

Mark it up to karma. It happens in business as it does in football and life. But you make your own luck, as the saying goes, luck being the intersection of being prepared when the opportunity arises. That's the payoff for being a responsible leader.

The worst (or funniest, depending on your point of view) coach reactions to watch are when a ref's call goes against them, because you can see steam about to come out of the coach's ears (see any montage of John Gruden or the khaki clad Michigan Wolverines coach Jim Harbaugh running down the sidelines shouting after a ref).

What's interesting to watch is how coaches handle the call, or how well they own the responsibility. And we all get it. NFL coaches are on the biggest stage in American sports and they only get 17 chances in a season to get it right. If they win two thirds of them they'll probably be in the playoffs. If they don't they're that much closer to the unemployment line and being a sub note in the annals of football history, so there's a lot on the line. Same goes for Division One college coaches.

In business it's the same, as well. Coaches and leaders who handle bad calls and defeat with grace and learn what not to do next time will have more success in the future, and their employees will want to stick around longer. People don't leave their job, they leave their leader. That's why it's not uncommon for players to give the "hometown discount" when they renegotiate a contract; they value where they are more than what they might earn somewhere else.

This is important because it ties back into the maxim that the vast majority of people want to be led, and they take their cues from the person out front. So if you want your people to be calm, especially during your two-minute drill, _you_ need to be calm.

Here are three examples of the importance of calm: a bad business call, a sad graduation send off, and one spectacular football drive.

- **Bad call.** Late in my HR career I worked in a distribution center (DC), quite often referred to by our corporate office as "the starship" because it was the newest and largest DC in the company. Expectations to produce were high. Because of that and the relatively close geographic proximity, we often had visitors down from corporate, making it an even more pressurized situation.

  What made things worse though was the regularity our GM would come out of his office after calls with his bosses shouting "EBITDA! EBITDA! EBITDA!", pacing up and down the suite's walkways in front of numerous admins, analysts and managers. His infamous rants created fertile ground for anxiety and all the trash that goes with it: siloed cliques, distrust, and fear that many felt during that period. Were we all on the chopping block as part of a drive to boost short-term earnings? We had our first union drive efforts at that time, a sure sign of detachment and disillusionment. No one was ever really comfortable and the building was never truly successful until he was moved on to a smaller DC (not a smart move by corporate—passing on a problem, but fortunate for our building).

- **Sad send-off.** Easily the most memorable portion of any speech I ever heard was at my sister Sara's high school graduation. It was a sad message with a great hook. The speaker, a gentleman certainly old enough to be the graduates' grandfather, said "Remember these two words; nine letters: 'Be careful.'" He went on to talk about how no matter what they chose to do, the most important thing to remember was to be careful.

Now to me being careful is typically a good thing, but unless you're working in a bomb squad or something equally danger-laden, "be careful" is probably not the primary concept you want to lead with or make your mantra; especially so for young people who have high aspirations. If your main message to your group is "be careful," you're not setting the stage for innovation or success.

Spectacular drive. Conversely, there's possibly no greater exam-ple of calm under pressure than the end of Super Bowl XXIII, when the San Francisco 49ers were down by a field goal to the Cincinnati Bengals. Quarterback Joe Montana had 3:10 left in the game to go 92 yards. As the team huddled to start the drive, backed up against its own end zone, Montana pointed into the crowd and said, "Hey, look, it's (actor) John Candy!" Joe was taking a poke at his lineman Harris Barton, who was always talking about famous people he saw.

Here's the magic of Joe's diversion: He was able to dial down the anxiety of a huge do-or-die situation for his teammates. And it paid off as they moved smoothly downfield to score the winning touchdown.

Spreading the benefits of "calm" is replicable at work. If you want employees in your store or department, or employees on the phone to be more cheery, you need to be cheery. If you want them to be more customer-service focused, you need to focus on serving both your customers AND employees better. State the goal and then go walk the talk. Regularly shouting "EBITDA!" around the troops does not help them improve EBITDA ratios!

Time at that DC wasn't always pretty, but life isn't always pretty. And thankfully we have workplace protocols, practices, and laws that keep organizations from (usually) abusing the system.

When we take a deep look at the most notable and respected coaches in football history (Nick Saban, Urban Meyer, Bill Walsh, Vince Lombardi, and Chuck Noll to name a few), many have written books or had books written about them, highlighting their methods. In a nutshell you can see that they all:

1. Trusted their system
2. Made their vision known to their players
3. Supported their players by coaching, listening, and communicating

A leader's maturity shows in how they react to the hand they're dealt at the beginning of the season as well as throughout the year regarding the overall status of the team. You can only do so much about the number of injuries, holdouts, and the quality of players (especially in key positions). It's not easy to have to work through the day-to-day muck of a swamp you're trying to drain. But it's a journey that must be made if you're going to build a winning team. These great coaches ultimately were winners both on the field and in the eyes of their players, because they owned the responsibility and led from the front.

Probably the ugliest situation is when the coach has lost control of his team; for whatever reason players have lost faith in him. Their anger and frustration are easy to see on the sidelines and are reflected in how they play. Coaches are already under pressure to win, but when they lose the respect and control of their players, it's typically going to be a short walk to the door.

Three of the things that I've learned through my career about leading people are that:

1. The vast majority of people want to be led, and
2. They usually want to be led from the front, and
3. They need clear and frequent communication.

That said, some leaders are more comfortable and effective when leading from behind. This type of leader may be more of a strategist and/or introvert, and they are typically quiet, technically minded people who have already established trust with their team and have strong performers on the field. Football examples include Jim Caldwell, Tony Dungy, Mike Tomlin, and Bill Snyder. But, importantly, even coaches who typically prefer to lead from behind do go out front from time to time to be seen and heard.

With all this said, if you truly want to change your team's culture, be patient. This kind of magic doesn't happen overnight, or in a few weeks, or even a few months. You need to go into this acting like it's an 80-yard drive for a touchdown. There will probably be penalties (setbacks) you'll have to deal with. The good thing is you probably aren't up against a clock winding down to 0:00 like Montana was. Be patient, be steady, be predicable for your team. Focus and communicate on the one thing you most want to change. If you can pull that off you'll be up for Coach of the Year!

I already mentioned one of the worst speeches ("Be Careful!") I ever heard. I didn't realize I had heard one of the best ones until days after I heard it.

I was at a conference in Atlanta and the keynote speaker was making the point that instead of asking someone how they were doing, he would say "Tell me something good." The difference he pointed out was that by asking someone how they were doing, you were inviting a litany of complaints, especially if you were talking to one of those actively disengaged people. You're just inviting a grievance about a mean-muggin', or something as small-minded. But by asking for something good, you're almost totally eliminating that negativity.

It wasn't until I returned home and was back at the office when I fell into my old habit: asking one of our malcontents how they were doing, just trying to keep positive communication flowing. After hearing an earful about how hot it was on the distribution floor, I walked away and BANG—finally had that epiphany about asking for something good. Huge difference maker, and one I always use now. Gotta keep those Donny and Debbie Downers from taking the air right out of the room, bringing down morale, and letting them control the culture.

One last point I'd like to make in this chapter deals with something I unfortunately see too much of: micro-managing.

I've come to learn *why* some people micro-manage (lack of confidence in their staff, which comes from a lack of or inflated sense of confidence in themselves). But it's up to top leadership to drive that out. The only time it might be necessary to micro-manage is when someone is brand-spanking new to the job that requires a special skill (such as running a lathe); or if there is a true crisis (fire in the warehouse!) when there isn't time for delegation, timing, and planning. Some might be tempted to micro-manage on a key project. But no one—no one—likes to be micro-managed. Not you, not me, not our employees.

So, how do you determine how much of a micro-manager you might be? Same way you determine your current culture: Ask someone you trust. Ask for a 360° review from the troops, handled through a mentor or trusted facilitator. Make it clear you want honest feedback to better yourself, so you can better the department. It's the Johari Window in action (description in the Listen chapter and the glossary). If you really want to make a difference, if you really want to be a great professional, you need to walk the talk.

Going to the Replay Booth

1. Leaders facilitate opportunity
2. In a leaderless vacuum, unscrupulous opportunists will seek power
3. Frequent communication and "walking the talk" is how you speed up culture change

CONTRIBUTOR ADDENDUM

Owning It – Rookie Survival to Veteran Success: Be a Pro

BY JEDIDIAH COLLINS, NEW ORLEANS SAINTS

(see page 118 for Jedidiah's bio and contact information)

Life is all about perspective, at times I would feel like a failure as I traveled from team to team through the NFL. Now, I can connect the dots backwards and feel fortunate to have entered 10 NFL locker rooms.

The adage heard in every building is more of a mindset than a saying—'Be a Pro.' What that means is that at this level, there is little room for excuse or error, simply get your job done—'Be a Pro!'

There are 3 factors in developing this mindset at a professional level:

1) Confident not Cocky

Every off season a new set of rookies show up and begin to tell everyone how good they were in college and how much they plan on making in the League. This cockiness is never received with its hopeful intentions. Young players are naïve to think veterans will listen and believe they can play. What so many overlook is that internal voice, the one between your ears, the one that is loudest when no one is around. This ability to believe in yourself and internally say "I can Be a Pro" is the first factor in becoming a professional athlete. The external voice is cockiness and leads nowhere, the internal voice is confidence and becomes your foundation. The first person that must believe you can, is you.

2) Team must Trust

In my first practice as a rookie, I lined up eager to prove I belonged. So excited, I couldn't wait for the ball to be snapped and jumped early. False start penalty and a mental error. Being the NFL, the whistle blew and I was replaced. Losing my rep and my first opportunity. Walking back to the sideline Coach Andy Reid said as I passed "We can't beat ourselves." With that Coach Reid shined a light on the second factor of being a pro—the team must trust me on the field. Trust that I will help the cause and not hurt it. Not knowing your assignment or committing a mental error is unacceptable at the professional level because it translates to your team not being able to trust you. Professionals do not beat themselves.

3) Make a Play

"I am from Missouri son, the Show-Me state," a common quote from an old running back coach and introduction to the most important factor of becoming a professional—Make a Play!

Down in the heat of a New Orleans August a veteran defensive lineman grabbed me after a play where I made a "chip" block. The veteran was understandably aggravated; not only was he battling the heat and the offensive tackle on the play, but I came by and "chipped" or threw my elbow into his ribs. Grabbing my facemask, the veteran barraged me with profanity and distinctly yelled out "I don't know you, I don't even know your name!"

With this comment, I had choices—cocky or confident. I could yell back at him and tell him my name or I could be confident. I could fight him and prove my toughness, but then I was showing a short fuse, one that couldn't be trusted.

One of the things I love about football is there will be another chance, a chance to make a play. The very next play my assignment was one on one with my new teammate and 300 lb. veteran Pro Bowl defensive end. On the snap of the ball, I came down the line and put my facemask right in the chest of this behemoth of a man, knocking him backwards and on to the ground. Walking up to him after the play, he expected an outreached hand to help him up, instead I merely tilted my helmet down and pointed to the tape on my across the front of my helmet—"Collins."

Without saying a word, I made a play and he knew my name.

As you approach the field, no matter if it is an NFL Stadium or corporate boardroom, begin to think "Be A Pro."

1. Believe you can do the job.
2. Don't beat yourself and earn the trust of your team.
3. Make me learn your name by adding value and making a play!

— 3 —

WEIGH

The W in "DOWN" stands for Weigh – the costs (of keeping vs. cutting – engaged vs. disengaged)

---

*"I have come here to chew bubblegum and kick ass.
And I'm all out of bubblegum."*

— RODDY PIPER
AS JOHN NADA, *THEY LIVE* (1988)

In the NFL, one of the toughest off-season decisions front offices have to make is who to keep and who to cut. Many factors come into play: Tangibles such as salary vs. the cap, past performance, likelihood of (re)injury, etc. Intangibles including locker room leadership and tendencies to blow-up like a knucklehead (see Adam "Pacman" Jones, Chad "Ochocinco" Johnson, Vontaze Burfict, and even some guys who didn't play in Cincinnati). In essence, the front office has to assess what value the player is bringing to the team.

Along similar lines, most business professionals have heard the stats on employees being engaged vs. disengaged, and the cost of disengaged employees. To recap, a Gallup Management Journal study that showed that less than 1/3 of US employees are "engaged" at work, with "engaged" meaning that they feel a passion for their work and a connection to their company. Over half are disengaged or "clocking-in and checking-out," and nearly 20% are actively disengaged—meaning they are purposefully NOT working or even working against the company! According to Gallup, highly engaged workforce companies outperform their peers by 147% in earnings per share. Total annual loss to the US economy is estimated in the hundred billions (yes, with a "b")! [2]

This study shows that when you break the workforce down:

- About 20% of the people (those who are engaged) typically show up before they're scheduled to be there, are strong workers, and are a joy to be around. You're happy they are on your team!

- A little more than half are not engaged, but they most often show up when they're supposed to and they do their work. Absolutely nothing wrong with these folks. They get the job done. Just don't expect much more than that.

- The remaining folks are actively disengaged, which means they spend their shift/energy wasting their and other peoples' time. There's nothing wrong with taking some breaks through the day and chatting at the water cooler, but these are the folks who go beyond that. Everyone else knows exactly who these time wasters are, and have to put up with it. Their number one wish is for you to take care of the situation.

Worth repeating: Your strongest performers' number one wish is for you to take care of the people who are pulling the team down. Obviously, the best way to get this done is to remove the actively disengaged people from the situation, which means to transfer them out or fire them. The problem with transferring them out is that you are then pushing your problem on some other poor, unsuspecting coach. Not a terribly ethical thing to do. That doesn't stop department leaders from doing it.

I would recommend that you step up and handle the situation more directly.

Remember that most recent behavior is the best predictor of future behavior. So when you're trying to figure out what to expect next from anyone, look at what they're currently doing.

One of the toughest things to do is to have to fire someone. But I would argue that even more difficult is keeping someone who is a bad fit. Just because they are a bad fit doesn't mean they are bad person, and you need to separate the two, which isn't easy for a lot of people to do. But hear me out on this. When there is a malcontent on your team, he or she is doing one thing well, and that thing is destroying the sense of team.

I'll never forget one worker who was one of those classic actively-disengaged employees. She was a total complainer, always stopping in our HR office, usually just as her shift started to complain about something minor.

The proverbial straw that broke the camel's back was when she walked straight into my office, unannounced, and said "You need to write up Reggie."

"For what?" I asked, looking up, wanting to rub the temples of my balding scalp.

"For mean-muggin' me."

She was a classic 20-percenter, taking up 80 percent of her department and the HR teams' time. Right after that incident I made an appointment with her department supervisors. We discussed her habitually poor behavior and the negative impact she brought to the area. Actually, I just facilitated the meeting, they were full of stories, anger, and frustration over her. So after letting them vent for a bit, we agreed to begin to document everything she did that caused a disturbance and they began to use our progressive discipline process. We figuratively stacked the box and game planned to use her behavior to get her out of the building. It took a many weeks, but she ended up losing her job. The supervisors learned how effective they could be working as a team on a thorny problem if they just used the tools they had at hand. And everyone, co-workers, supervisors, and me, were much happier when she was gone.

I usually joke that it's the HR investigations I ran that caused the early onset of my baldness—that includes cheek-licking incidents, serial-lunch stealers, and commenting on the color of thong underwear, as well as those reports of mean-muggings. But your hairline is less important than losing strong employees who leave the team because you won't take action on an ongoing personnel problem.

The character of your team will ultimately determinate its level of success. A strong leader can only do so much with mediocre talent. Work skills (how to drive a forklift, designing blueprints, giving presentations, etc.) can be taught. Character can't. That means the level of grit, passion, willingness to learn, and acceptance of diversity should always be considered when selecting team members.

In HR terms: Hire slowly and deliberately.

There are many reasons why you could have malcontents in your midst. It could be that they feel they've been overlooked. They could be misplaced, meaning their skills would be much better suited elsewhere. Or they could just be a bad egg.

I would argue that you owe it to them to find which is the real situation, at least as they see it. If they are frustrated in their job, you owe it to yourself and them as a good leader to find out their history. If the person has been passed over repeatedly, ask yourself and those who made that decision, why? If they are a competent employee, give them the proper training so they can move forward. Be sincere about it, by letting them know that you've looked at the situation, done a gap analysis, and see this training helping them to close that gap.

It may be that the malcontents are highly skilled but just in the wrong position. That could happen for a number of reasons, but most likely they just found themselves in this job and are working through it, but are not happy about it, and therefore causing disruptions.

You certainly wouldn't put someone who is adept at working on cars in charge of your website, would you? This mismatch is on the organization, not so much on them. Again, an honest conversation with them about their true passions and professional goals would help.

I'm a big believer in the Myers-Briggs type indicator (MBTI) or DiSC, two relatively inexpensive methods to find out where people might be a good fit. For under $100 you can perhaps solve this problem using MBTI, and get them into a better situation they are better suited for, hopefully within your organization so that you keep a good person, even if she or he were displaced originally.

Once in a long while you'll find you're dealing with someone who is in the doghouse because of one bad mistake. Overall they've been a reliable or even solid contributor. But one bad happenstance occurred—maybe an oversight that put a big hurt on the bottom line, an overreach of their area of responsibility, or a release of proprietary information. These are difficult calls, but like the ref who is in the replay booth *for-ever*, you want to get it spot-on correct.

Underlying character certainly somehow needs to be assessed when giving someone a second chance. Again, I'll point you back to the maxim that the most recent behavior is an indicator of who they are. Nothing is sweeter than redemption, and no one is more faithful than someone given a chance to redeem themselves. That, along with underlying character, should carry a lot of weight when you are trying to decide on how to handle them.

The last possibility is the most concerning: You just have a bad egg. How they got in, who knows. But you need to get rid of them. Your people are begging you to do it. Maybe not to your face, but certainly behind your back. It would be the best holiday gift you could give the department. So, what do you do?? You begin to do what you are there for, solve problems. This is probably one of the biggest problems in your department: handling a malcontent. So you get with your buddies in human resources and you begin to work it out.

I am unlike most HR people I've met, and it's probably because I don't have a lot of patience. Good or bad, I have never seen the rationale for keeping an underachiever. Consider this: If a person isn't performing it's because of one of two things:

1. Either you didn't train the employee properly on how to do the job, or
2. She or he is refusing to do the job properly.

In those situations, you should first acknowledge to them that perhaps you or your predecessor didn't do your job well, and that you will re-train them so that they can be a contributor. After thoroughly going over the person's job description, then literally showing them how to do it, and both agreeing that they know how to do it; you document the conversation and let them run back out there to the job.

If they are now successful, you know you have to sharpen your managing/training/orientation skills. But if they are not succeeding, you need to have a crucial conversation with them about what they are doing wrong—and have them show you step-by-step what they are supposed to do. (I'll bet that they can.) Document the conversation, and let them run back out there again. If they fail this time—cut the employee.

"Whoa!" a lot of people tend to say at that. "Cut him? Fire her?!? You can't do that; it's illegal and/or unethical. That's just being an unfeeling boss; its draconian—that's what's wrong with companies!" In football words they're ready to throw a flag for a flagrant personal foul.

And my response?? Listen to this: Disengaged employees cost America around $500B/year. Billion. As in 11 zeros after the dollar sign. $500,000,000,000. Disengaged employees lower other employees' morale. Disengaged employees cost you more to keep than if you made a gutsy call, phoned your Director of HR (and/or local employment law attorney) and invited the person to the door.

And here's how:

Hopefully you catch the problem within the employee's probationary period. As long as you go through the steps outlined in your policies and handbook you should be fine letting the person go.

But let's say that the problem child has been around longer. Maybe even waaaay longer; their probationary period is what followed the Mesozoic Period. They may know where the bodies are buried. Heck, they may be the one *burying* the bodies. But they are poison. They spend more time figuring out how NOT to work than they do working.

There are two ways you can go about it: 1) the slow painful way of corrective actions, hoping you cross your T's and dot your I's correctly; or 2) the quick, yank-the-arrow-from-your-butt (ala "Shrek") method. One quick, "big hurt" move sends a message to the team that "we're no longer putting up with this!" This "big hurt" may mean you'll be digging in your pockets a bit for legal support and/or a separation package, but in the long run it's far more cost effective.

(Now I will give you the caveat that if you work in a union shop or are a government employer you are probably less able to use the "big hurt" method. But remember, if you have a union shop, then at some point in your company's history you probably deserved it. Oh, and, yeah, I am not a labor lawyer so you should not take what I say for legal guidance.)

Towards the end of my HR days I was so disillusioned with my boss and work place that I made a game out of handling terminations. My secret challenge was to have done such a good job of building a case supporting the *employee's* ambitions that they would be thanking me and shaking my hand as they were leaving the building.

It basically started the way it often does, with a manager complaining about someone missing time, not following rules, having marginal productivity, etc. I'd ask if they had been taking corrective action, and usually the answer was "no, I'm too busy." So we'd close the door and begin to outline the problem as specifically as the manager and her leads could legitimately recall. Then I'd ask the manager and leads to tell me about the employee's interests and goals. Again, rarely could I get a very specific picture.

Because we were in a distribution center we were usually able to determine numbers that supported the claim. Again, it was rarely solid evidence, but if there was enough smoke to convince me we had a fire, I would lay my groundwork for operation "Get the Bad Out."

Their manager and I would then call the employee in to go over numbers and our concerns, outlining acceptable goals. At the end of the conversation I would ask the employee what they were most interested in doing work-wise. Sometimes it was a position in the DC, but more often they were biding time before something better came along. We had a sincere conversation, because in all honesty I was interested in creating a win-win situation, whether that meant they stayed or left the DC. And so for 10 minutes the employee, manager and I talked about dreams and plans to get there, and helped them see how they could work a path to that goal.

Now at this point one of three things would happen.

The first is that the employee was smart enough to see that we might have intentions on showing them the door and they would immediately start meeting standards. When that is the case, that's great, because the employee is now working hard and the manager learns something very personal, near-and-dear to them, and the employee and manager can talk about that on the floor. And so can I when I see that employee on the floor or in the common areas.

The second possibility is that the point doesn't sink in and the employee continues to struggle to meet whatever the standard is. And we would keep meeting, and talking more and more about them chasing their dream. Eventually we'd have a final meeting that went something like:

> Me: Now we've met several times,
>
> Employee (EE): yeah…
>
> Me: and I know you know we're not happy with your work performance,
>
> EE: yeah…
>
> Me: and I know you're not that happy here; you'd rather be _____ (their passion) _____ .
>
> EE: yeah…
>
> Me: So here's what we're going to do. We're going to terminate your time here, but you'll be leaving with xx vacation days, xx sick days, and here's what I'm going to do—we're getting you a session with a job coach [cost: free – $200] who's going to work on your resume and help you jump into the _____ field. [Looking them in the eye] You are set to take off! In a while you'll be looking back at this and be laughing at me still being stuck here!
>
> EE: (Laughing, extending hand to shake) Thank you, thank you Mr. Rod.

This scenario actually happened several times. It was during this period that we had a new head of security come on (Jake), and one of the first things Jake told me was that he was going to sit in on every termination meeting I had. I told him that he wasn't, but he could stand outside the door if he wanted.

I'll never forget the first time he was standing outside: I completed the unfortunate deed and the now ex-employee left my office giving me multiple thank-you's and a smile. Jake—who was a BIG guy—could barely control his laughter.

"What did you do?" he asked.

"Simple" I replied. "We had several talks before. Both he and I knew he was disengaged—but we discussed why he was disengaged and how it would be best for him to find a place where he could fulfill his passion. We both recognized that it wasn't here so he saw it as we were solving a problem for him. And while he may temporarily be out of a job, he's feeling good about himself and has a much better sense of direction and purpose."

AND—even better perhaps—morale in your department will skyrocket. You may even hear thank-you's from your employees.

So, a win-win situation. Congratulations, you just swept a double-header. (Wrong sport, I know, but you get the idea.)

The third possibility (that occasionally happened) is that the employee became SO inspired with our talk about their active disengagement that they'd quit within a few days—problem gone!

(One last thought. I should note that there may be a fourth possibility: they just aren't capable of grasping the job itself, in which case you still should show them the door or demote them to a job they can handle, like water boy.)

Go to the Replay Booth

1. If a personnel situation isn't working out it's for one of two reasons. The first is that you didn't train the person properly.

The second is that you did train them properly and they are simply refusing to do the job. Again, you have to first assume that you are the one at fault.

2. HR is a good group with which to develop a strong relationship. When problems do arise, it will be easier to muddle through those personnel issues with a friendly face with knowledge and proven processes to support you.

4

NEGOTIATE

The N in "DOWN" stands for Negotiate – your final roster (top young talent, projects, free agents, and vets)

"Hey Johnny, what are you rebelling against?"

"What have you got?"

—MARLON BRANDO
AS JOHNNY STRABLER, *THE WILD ONE* (1953)

Marlon's line, "What have you got?" is a really good question you should be asking yourself when you start leading a team—what exactly have you got *talent-wise*?

Obviously a team's success rests a lot on the effectiveness of the players on the current roster.

The trick is to determine exactly what you have as quickly as you can. If possible, I recommend that before starting the job that you learn the <u>exact</u> responsibilities of your department. And from that I urge that you decide what positions that, in a perfect world, you'd have in place.

Assuming you are going into a new situation (essentially taking over a team), it would be a huge benefit for you to research what you have *before you even decide to accept the position.* That's why, along with asking in your interview about the work flow process, you need to ask about the employees.[3] The person interviewing you may not know the details of the department's personnel situation, but without pressing them too much it is good to ask for whatever details they can offer. The more you know before going in, the fewer surprises you'll have to contend with once you land the position. Knowledge is power! The more you know why something is the way it is and the people involved, the better prepared you will be to handle the big issues and the unique quirks that you will ultimately run into.

At your first round of interviews ask the hiring manager, the HR rep, the people who will be your peers, clients, and suppliers this question: "What is the reputation of this team—and of the specific members—that I'm taking over?"

Also in your interview, it would be good to ask about the exact parameters for the area's workflow. With this information you should draw in your own mind a best-case scenario. You might see the need for one administrative assistant, a part-time employee, a specialist, two generalists, and a manager, all based on workflow needs. Then compare that to what the organization actually has in place. You can even apply a Gap Analysis to this. And for everything that differs, ask why it is set up differently. Doing so will show you the specific history of the area you're going into.

There are probably some good (or not so good) reasons why the department looks different than what you would imagine. It could relate to the money budgeted for the area, or people who have been placed there for specific reasons (you may be now managing the CEO's girlfriend!), or the general ineptitude of your predecessor.

Aside from the department's work flow process, get a copy of its organization chart. After the interview, study it to see if the processes make sense and the personnel are there to execute them. It very well may be fine as is, but you should always look to tweak (continuous improvement). From that tweaking, an opportunity for growth for some personnel may emerge.

Whatever the reason for the current status, it's good for you to know why it is shaped differently than what you envision as a best-case scenario. There could be very good reasons as to why it is organized the way it is. This interview would be a fantastic opportunity to learn the "whys" of the organization's processes.

On your second interview you can do a deeper dive: What are the specific strengths and weaknesses of the team members, their professional goals (do they want to stay in the field, industry, company) and their training needs? What is the makeup of the talent? Does the department have any generalists? Does it need any? If there are some, do any have an interest in becoming a specialist? If so, is it in an area of need or is the department already stacked in specialists?

Ask about the overall personality of the team, the culture, why it is that way, and who the unofficial leaders are. And why. The more intel you can get on all the players on your team, the better able you will be to immediately step in, anticipate what is going to happen, and set a new direction. And here's a big benefit: If need be, you will be better able to avoid any hot water that might be waiting for you to step in on day one—preemptive moves to not become a scalded frog.

Based on the feedback you collected you should literally plot on a chart what you have—broken into rookies, stars, specialists, weak links. The HR managers may even have a succession plan based on their synopsis of the department. You should ask for a copy of that. (And if there's not one, after you've been there for a year you should ask someone in HR to help you create one!)

When you have been hired for the position and finally meet your new group, you need to plan in your first few days to have heart-to-heart conversations with each one to find out how they feel about being on the team as well as their career path, and how you can assist, even if it means they would rather be out. Even if they are a productive employee. Your job as a great leader is to keep the good, productive employees, fix the issues regarding the disengaged employees, and assist those who want change into getting out or moving up.

Based on how your research goes, you can literally draw up a diagram/ org chart showing your current situation. You can then ask yourself, based on the responsibility of my area:

- what talent do we need?
- what talent can we get?
- what talent would be better if it were gone? and
- how can we bridge that?

It might be that you're coming from a great system that you can replicate at your new employer. If you were doing the job with six well-trained employees, do you really need the eight this prospective employer has? Or if they only have four, can you make the argument that you need one more if the work loads are similar?

In the case where you've been the manager of a team for a while, you may feel you may know the answer to this already. But I'll point you back to the Frog Soup story: You may have been in the warming pot long enough that you don't have the clearest view of the team. So take the same action—ask the people who are your peers, clients, and suppliers this: "What is the reputation of this team - and of the specific members?"

And how does that translate into negotiating your final roster? Rarely does a boss get to pick who is on their team. Chance dictates that you inherit a group in any of several possible states of cohesion and effectiveness.

Professional sports teams have to negotiate with players, or, more correctly, with the players' agents (unless you are Lamar Jackson). Owners and GMs strive to create a team they want to move forward with. Workplace America doesn't work that way, but there is still the opportunity to try to create what you want.

Just as any professional (or college, for that matter) team assesses what their roster talent and holes are, you need to do the same. And just like in the NFL, you are probably dealing with some sort of a salary cap. It's not like you can just go down to the GM's office and say, "Hey boss, I needs me a backup QB and a special teamer" (or more likely an accountant and clerk). But you can get inventive to a degree if necessary.

Reflect back on the W in DOWN and management expert Jim Collin's metaphor about the need to have the right people in the right seats on the bus: Sometimes you may find you're dealing with a person who doesn't fit in. Again, the best thing you can do in my opinion is to get the person off the bus as fast as you can. I don't see this as being hard-hearted.

There are lots of "buses" (organizations) out there, each with its own culture. If you like your culture and someone truly doesn't fit in, you're creating a win-win by getting them out the door. (But you should help them hail a new bus with, at minimum, time with a career counselor who can update their resume.)

If you aren't new to your position and therefore already in the flow of things, you may know where there's other talent in the company you could attempt to bring over to your team. It might require some fina-gling, but it's doable.

That's right, instead of looking outside the company, look inside to add better players to your team.

One of the truths I've learned about the workplace is wherever there is high turnover, it's probably directly under a manager who has poor relations with their staff. Again, people mostly don't leave their job, they leave their boss. So if there's a weak manager in the company, some-one with a less than stellar reputation, there may be people looking to bail from that department. They may think a transfer is a great option. Granted there could be a number of variables (are wages equivalent, skills transferable, etc.?) but it's worth looking into if you need more/

better talent. You ultimately want a team where everyone is passionate about and good at what they do.

When you have devised a solid plan and rationale, ask those employees in the other department if they'd be interested in a move over to your area. If they are, then discuss that plan with HR on how to get them transferred. Mention to the HR manager that the employee has expressed an interest and said they would be happier in your area. The HR manager may be surprised at your forwardness, but probably won't be surprised to hear someone wants to leave an area with a weak or bad manager.

Negotiate a plan with them involving HR on how to get them where they would be happier. Negotiate a plan to hire a replacement, or to make a business case to add a position, or to trade a redundant position for a different opening.

I would be remiss if I didn't mention looking at nontraditional sources for finding good employees. You see this all the time in the NFL when teams scour the CFL, other practice teams, and small colleges for more players. One real-life instance that stands out to me is when we hired a Jim, a former convict, for our security team. Counter intuitive? Sure, but if you're trying to stop theft, having a reformed thief on your team can be very helpful.

Just a few weeks into joining our team, he caught an equipment handler trying to steal some laptops a client reported missing. Jim had a good hunch where the handler hid them before trying to sneak them out of the building later that week!

A quick, personal story to illustrate the importance of having a strong, diverse roster:

> When my wife and I bought our first house we had ended up working with a Realtor named Ned. Ned was built like a barrel, almost as wide as he was tall. You could tell he played football long before he "girthed out," and his personality

matched his waistline; it was big. But we liked him; he came across as thorough and confident.

Throughout the process he'd regale us with stories of his former playing days and current coaching dramas. While much of it came off as wistful bluster of days gone by, he told one humorous story that stuck out to me. It was about how his most recent team had just won the championship game. They had a good offense and defense, but their formula for winning was using a trio of very different running backs. He even gave each one a nickname: "Flea," "Trek," and "Dozer". Flea was small and fast, kind of like former Chargers/Eagles star Darrin Sprole: He could hide and dash. He was fast and hard to track down, and would tire people out trying to chase him down. After a while Ned would put in Trek, who was a somewhat larger guy with a chip on his shoulder. Much like receiver former Panthers/Ravens star Steve Smith in spirit, he talked a tough game and backed it up with his play. And late in the third quarter came Dozer, who of course was the big bruiser, like former Houston Oilers star Earl Campbell, who no one felt like trying to handle after facing the first two.

It's important to point out that (obviously) not all your employees are equally talented, and that means you need to be conscientious with how you are deploying their skill sets. English management guru Meredith Belbin has written that a team of specialists will almost always out-perform a team of solid "jack-of-all-trades." Top football teams are full of specialists. You too may have these specialists on your team who are tasked with getting specific jobs done. On football teams the coaches work with these specialists on how to tackle particular obstacles (such as how to handle a defensive bull rusher larger than you, or how to handle a QB who can run as well as throw.)

Ned's story was both humorous and on target. His point is the same as Belbin's, that a team of specialists will almost always beat a team of generalists. (You can see a good whiteboard animation on YouTube about Belbin's concept; it shows that there are nine possible roles a person can play.)

Conversely, a "jack of all trades" may be good as a stop-gap in a pinch, but you're not going to win the Super Bowl with a team full of them, much less make the play-offs.

What are you doing to work with your specialists to help them get your team ahead?? Are you truly doing all that you can to facilitate opportunity for them—letting them focus on what they're good at and passionate about so they can kick that winning field goal as time expires?

One example I can share about flipping a generalist to a specialist (or at least developing a new special skill) is when I was managing that HR department in the large (1,000+ employee) distribution center. We were letting a number of unemployment claims go uncontested for people who were released for poor performance, theft, attendance, etc. Doesn't sound like a huge deal, but it was definitely hitting our bottom line because the warehouse had such a high turnover and my team was treading water in paperwork already.

So I took one of our budding clerks and trained her how to do investigations, work with managers on performance issues, and prepare for sitting through an unemployment hearing. I even took her on some hearings to see firsthand how they ran.

My director scoffed at first but when we started seeing a drop in the money we were losing, he changed his tune. The work the clerk was originally doing was now handled in part by a lead from the floor who had shown promise and interest in getting out of operations and into HR. So we were saving money while giving two growth opportunities to a couple of 20-somethings. That's like a three-game winning streak, which is very nice to have!

Check now for how you are doing. Make two lists of all your employees, breaking them into either a generalist or specialist category:

MY GENERALISTS	MY SPECIALISTS

Compare this list to the needs you have. How well do they match up? Any disconnect you see—that's one of your key jobs to fix!

To close, remember that dynasties don't happen overnight, and they don't happen by chance or luck. They are intentionally put together. As you intentionally pull yours together, identify the stars, specialists, high potentials, place holders and weak links. Focus on the weak links; can you turn them into keepers? If not, design a plan to move them on and/ or out. Are there any employees outside of your team you can pick up? Make plans for that too. Base your decisions on efficient work flow. Tie your employees' ambitions to your needs. If you have plans they fit into, let them know. Set goals for them that fill your team's needs.

Go to the Replay Booth

1. Look at the group's org chart and compare it to the work flow and the area's responsibilities. Does it make sense? If not, make a case for change.
2. Keep the keepers and get rid of those who aren't good fits. In a loving, win-win way.

CONTRIBUTOR ADDENDUM

Negotiations

BY JEFF DIAMOND,
MINNESOTA VIKINGS AND TENNESSEE TITANS

(see page 119 for Jeff's bio and contact information)

During my 20 plus years as an NFL Vice President/General Manager with the Minnesota Vikings and President/COO of the Tennessee Titans, I negotiated all kinds of deals—including contracts with players and coaches through their agents, player trades, stadium leases, broadcasting agreements, sponsorship deals, and injury settlements.

In recent years, I have negotiated for clients as CEO of a government relations firm and for many other clients including my current work for the NFL agent group IFA. I advise the other agents in our firm on negotiating strategy for our players, so I've worked on both the management and labor side of the negotiating table.

My negotiating skills were put to an extreme test during a two-year stretch in 1998 and 1999 that was a great example of the roller coaster world of professional sports (similar to most businesses).

As VP/GM of the '98 Vikings, I had helped build a powerhouse team that peaked in that season and I had successfully negotiated new contracts with several star players who we were in danger of losing via free agency. We soared to a 15-1 season—best record in the NFL—but we lost a heartbreaking NFC Championship Game in overtime to Atlanta.

I was selected NFL Executive of the Year following that season so it seemed that I was in a great position to get a big new deal in Minnesota with my contract up. I was negotiating my own deal—a huge challenge with the emotion involved—but I became embroiled in a power struggle with our head coach who wanted to take over my GM role along with his coaching duties and we had a new owner who didn't fully appreciate my contributions.

It became apparent that I needed to extricate myself from a negative situation at the height of my personal success and make sure I had the right final roster of support staff, coaches and players in my next job or as stated in this Negotiation chapter—"the right people in the right seat on the bus" (which was no longer the case with the Vikings).

I had offers from several teams and as difficult as it was to leave my hometown team and uproot my family, I decided there were better opportunities elsewhere and it was time (as Jim Collin says) to find a new bus.

I was intrigued by the best offer financially and from a career-path standpoint which was to become Titans President/COO. My family and I would be moving from our northern roots to the mid-south which sounded great weather-wise but was a big culture change. In researching this opportunity, I understood it was a huge plus that the Titans were moving into a new stadium in downtown Nashville and a state-of-the-art practice facility/offices, which were major upgrades over what we had in Minnesota and would be attractive to free agent players along with coaches and other staff.

I analyzed the Titans' roster, talked with friends around the league who worked in player personnel, and determined that the team had the potential to be elite with a few tweaks that I could help bring about.

I spoke with a media friend who covered the team and knew the organization's inner workings. He told me of team owner Bud Adams' history of falling in and out of love with his top execs, suggesting I seek a long term contract. He warned me of a power struggle going on between the GM Floyd Reese and Head Coach Jeff Fisher involving Reese having control over Fisher's coaching staff hires. I also learned from my research that the Nashville and the middle Tennessee market were football-crazy and there was plenty of corporate and season ticket support. So the opportunity was too good to pass up, I signed a four-year contract to give me sufficient time to help turn an 8-8 team into a Super Bowl contender.

After the way things ended with the Vikings, I wanted to be sure I had the best possible support at all levels—execs, football and business side staff, coaches, and players. In my first days on the job, I had conversations with Reese, Fisher and player leaders such as our star running back Eddie George to receive input on how they felt the organization could improve in supporting the team. Based on their insights and my own early observations, I convinced Bud Adams that we would send a strong internal message by going to a higher level of operating first class with team travel logistics, providing nutritious team meals at no cost in the facility on practice/meeting days, and to do what we had to do contract-wise to keep our best players and build an excellent team around them.

Another immediate step was to sit down with a talented GM in Reese who excelled in player evaluation and with Fisher who was a head coach with a good reputation, which I learned from speaking with qualified people in the organization and around the league. I wanted to quickly clarify their roles since I had negotiated that responsibility in my contract. I held the leverage in these discussions and I told Reese and Fisher that I wanted them to stay long term but if they wouldn't work effectively together then one or both of them would have to move on because it was tough enough to win in the ultra-competitive NFL with everyone pulling together and virtually impossible to be successful if that wasn't the case.

It helped with Reese that he and I were long-time friends going back to when he was an assistant coach with the Vikings early in our careers. I told him that while I was ultimately in charge and I would be the point person on salary cap management and assist him on star player negotiations as per my expertise, I would delegate to him control over player evaluation and acquisition (via the draft and free agency). I also said I wanted he and I to work closely with Fisher to get the coaching staff input on current players' abilities and potential additions.

I also told Reese that he no longer would have the power to veto Fisher's coaching staff hires as I thought the best course was for the head coach to sink or swim with his assistant coach choices. But I told Fisher that I expected him to accept input from Reese in this area since Reese had been a long-time coach in the league prior to his time as an assistant GM and now a GM.

As I emphasize in my current college and corporate speeches on negotiation, I had done my research on the situation, I acted professionally and treated both men with respect. I was tough but fair and understood power and leverage—which I had in these negotiations—but didn't want to abuse it. And I always kept in mind my main motto in negotiations: Be easy on people and hard on the problem.

Reese and Fisher both agreed to my organizational strategy and the three of us worked well together for the next five years to create a unified top of the organization that I believe played a significant role—of course along with our talented players—in leading to the franchise's first-ever Super Bowl appearance in my first season (1999) and three more playoff seasons to follow. It was the highlight of my NFL career to reach the Super Bowl with the Titans after falling short the year before in Minnesota.

After five years with the Titans, I left after a contract dispute with Adams who was happy with my performance but no longer wanted to pay me my market value. I then decided to take on a new challenge with my consulting, media, and speaking work.

PSST – let's take a quick TO – 'cause this is an important piece

I often get asked "what can I do if I have a crappy boss?" It's a tenuous situation because it can not only have a negative effect on your work life but impact and affect your *entire* life. And the frustration level can be higher if you actually like the company. *It's just that damn boss!!*

The problem is that you can't just wish the situation away. You can pray for it, but that bus isn't going to hit them as they're crossing the street tomorrow. And Karma may be a bitch, but she also usually takes a looooong time to show up to the party. Meanwhile you're going through hell.

The unfortunate truth is that while you may be a talented, dedicated employee who is right as rain, if you have just three stripes on your sleeve and your boss has five, you will <u>always</u> lose. You may be a four-year starter and captain of the team, but your coach will always be the one making the play call. It could be your boss has made the big boss blind or apathetic to the flotsam and jetsam they're they are leaving in their wake. But as long as they are seen as getting results, their boss will probably not care or act on his poor performance immediately. It's only when your boss' behavior gets so bad that their boss can't take the embarrassment anymore that anything will change.

If you are in this position you have my sympathy. As I see it you have three choices:

1. **Make a sideways (lateral) move so you can stay with the organization.** Remember in this last section talking about negotiating your team...this is the opposite side of the coin. You can be that free agent looking to jump ship; drop playing for that horrible coach, and move to a well-run team.

2. **If you're facing illegal/harassing behavior, go to HR.** But you better have plenty of documentation. And remember,

there's a difference between illegal behavior and unethical behavior. It unfortunately is not illegal to be a total jerk to your employees. Depending on the organization's culture (especially in HR and the amount of power the HR Director has) you may not get much traction, sympathy, or a positive outcome.

3. **Leave the organization.** Especially tough to do if you like the organization but just hate the boss.

On a creative note, my mentor Tom once shared a story of a time early in his career when he and his co-workers were suffering through a horrible boss, Joyce. When a position one step above Joyce on the org chart opened they hoped she would apply for it, but for some reason she did not. So they went ahead and wrote a letter of support for Joyce, all signed it, and sent it to the division director. From that letter she was personally invited and encouraged to apply by the division director. Joyce changed her mind, applied for, and landed the job. Voila, problem solved!

Now I'm not saying that's necessarily the most ethical move to pull, but it did solve their problem!

Reviewing DOWN

So the first steps are to **Determine** the culture you want—something you can do even before going into the organization. Be honest with yourself—what is your natural "go to" mode. How can you make that work for a team of people who aren't disengaged? And remember to do your homework on the group's recent history of leadership and followership.

You must and will be expected to **Own** the responsibility of leader as soon as you meet your team. They are looking for you to give them a message and direction and they will be able to tell soon enough how capable you are of delivering.

After a short period of time you will be able to tell who is engaged and who is disengaged. **Weigh** the costs of who to keep, who to try to engage, and who to cut. Work with HR to get your plan of action going.

In doing so you will have **Negotiated** your final roster.

Now go get 'em, Tiger!

PART TWO

SET

The Stance and Pick the Right Posture

5

SELL

The S in "SET" stands for Sell, as in the vision. Specifically the vision of your organization, or area, or team, depending on how high up the pecking order you are.

"I love the smell of napalm in the morning."

—ROBERT DUVALL AS LIEUTENANT COLONEL
WILLIAM "BILL" KILGORE, *APOCALYPSE NOW*
(1979)

In *Apocalypse Now*, Duvall's character, Lt. Col. Bill Kilgore, is memorable, in part because he had clear standards and objectives, and because he worked to create a team that lived and fought according to those clear standards and objectives. He sold his team a vision of how war should be fought and life should be lived. It was a tough movie about a tough, often divisive topic. My point is that nodes of excellence can exist within an organization that is not as focused on excellence or is not achieving excellence.

There's an old adage that a team's style of play reflects their head coach. You see this in sports from U-10 rec soccer (fun coach!) to the NFL (Seahawks coach Pete Carroll's free-wheeling). The topic has been covered in numerous ways, from books about famed Packer's coach Vince Lombardi to podcasts about Steelers coach Mike Tomlin.

Drawing from this case, the truth is that even a manager of just three employees or volunteers can set a tone different from the rest of the organization. On NFL teams you can break it down from a team of 53 players to just the defense and then zero in on the linebackers. As of when I'm writing this, the Baltimore Ravens list 28 coaches on their team's website, from Head Coach to Assistant Strength & Conditioning coach to Kicking Consultant to Football Information Manager (whatever that is). The point is, each of these people can create their own sub-cultures within the team, just as you can in your organization. In fact, they may have their own reputation within an organization that has a similar but slightly different reputation. (Think of a security department in an urban hospital: The guards set a no-nonsense presence in an organization that promotes caring and wellness.)

Reflect on an organization you've been involved with. Identify which managers have a great reputation. Now think about their teams—do they have a clear idea of what their mission is? Probably. Chances are they are both an effective and relatively happy group. That doesn't just happen though; it's because the team has a vision that's been bought into, and repeated (or sold) again and again and again.

Driving home this point, think of your last three managers (or one or two if you are newer in the world of work or haven't had different managers). Think about their clarity of organizational mission and the overall performance of their team.

Most recent 3 managers and level of clarity

1. _____

2. _____

3. _____

Now name the three best managers you've ever had and do the same:

1. _____

2. _____

3. _____

What conclusions are you drawing? I'm going to bet that the clearer the mission, the better the performance. Granted that doesn't necessarily translate into a happy, fulfilled team, but it was probably effective.

The opposite is true; if you have a poorly planned culture or don't put forth any effort to intentionally create a strong, supportive, positive culture, you'll have a weak team. Garbage in, garbage out.

I worked for a company that had lots of outlet stores. While the culture at headquarters was pretty good, all those stores were basically at the mercy of the strength of their respective managers. Some were great, some were good, and some had me flying out to do investigations on harassment claims (including those cheek licking and thong-commenting incidents I mentioned earlier). Yes, truth is stronger than fiction. If I were to write a book on all claims I investigated, I think the title will be something like _What Were You Thinking_?! It's all about eliminating an environment that turns a blind eye to bad behavior, or worse, encourages it.

Intentional communication is key. Studies show that managers who have well run regular team meetings also enjoy higher morale; poorly led meetings can kill it, though. No coincidence there. Regular meetings are the perfect opportunity to SELL the overall message. Review the KPIs (Key Performance Indicators) that count. Point out the advantages of doing things in a certain way, of organizations with similar approaches and the successes they enjoy.

If you wanted to get deeper buy-in, gather your team to sit and talk about how they can become better together. Bring up your Vision and Mission statements (if you have them). Discuss how together you can collectively be intentional about your future and how to innovate.

Lots of organizations have Vision Statements—essentially thoughtful goals based on the values of the organization. Some of the best ones (in my opinion) include:

1. "To be remembered as the company that brought science to the art of marketing." (Data Xu)

2. "To fulfil dreams through the experiences of motorcycling." (Harley Davidson)

3. "Be recognized as a preeminent global engineered-materials and services company that fully engages our people, passionately embraces new ideas, seeks out transforming technologies and operates with unbending ethical standards." (PPG Industries)

But why can't a division, department, or even a person have a Vision Statement?? They can! And by getting a group to focus on that Vision Statement you can get your people to focus on a simple axiom that everyone can rally around.

You could even take it a step farther and create a logo, symbol, mascot and/or totem for your team. When teams run out on the field for a game, many (especially college teams) will pass by and touch a statue of their mascot, or touch a sign posted above the exit onto the field. In Baltimore, the sign reads "Play like a Raven." In Las Vegas, it says "Commitment to Excellence." They are reminders to players that the symbol or message represents the values of the organization. It instills pride and motivation.

So why can't you post a saying over the copier, a picture of a bulldog on the door, or a duck decoy from the garden store in your lunch area? Or if you're in a mostly virtual organization, add an fox theme to your internal messages? So many things can come from it. (Think "bulldog award" for best productivity, or a service dog for receiving a customer service kudos.) You can create virtually anything to identify yourselves as a team with a purpose, represented by a slogan or animal. and create some fun around it. The thing about it is

You need to be intentional about it.

You need to have a clear picture going in of what you want to accomplish. This is your chance to reset the culture of your area, so do it with purpose, create a vision, and sell it. Explain the "why" for doing it. It could be you want to focus on one or two specific things. (Don't do any more than three. if you do, you'll dilute the vision and targets.)

Want to turn a reputation around? Want to stand out? Want to prove something to the rest of the organization? Create your vision and sell it.

One organization I was in wanted to increase morale and encourage us to get to know one other better. We had just gone through a re-org, and few people were happy about it. Someone brought in a small rubber duck fashioned to look like a pirate. People were encouraged to pass it around when they saw someone do something good (with a short note explaining why they got the duck). The person who got the duck was responsible for passing it on within a week to a co-worder with a note.

After a couple of weeks, we all received an email from one of our co-workers who had taken the duck to a conference and took pictures of the duck in a variety of settings: on top of the conference binder, next to a workshop sign, at the pool bar next to a colorful drink. Suddenly everyone was commenting on the duck and people asked to reserve the duck so they could take it to a conference months later. There was a contest to give the duck a name ("Booty" was decided on, insert your own Booty jokes here:_____). The duck became a conversation starter, if it went on a conference, the person taking it there had to talk to the group about what they learned while away. Over the course of about six months Booty helped increase morale. (Ok, enough of the Booty jokes now.)

- By "selling it" you are letting everyone know what you're doing and WHY you're doing it.
- Our quality is down, so we're going to think more like hawks—very focused

- Our customer service metrics are down, so we're going to think more like border collies—walking alongside them very attentively
- We need to up our creativeness, so we're going to think more like foxes—cunning
- We need to up productivity, so we're going to think more like bees—industrious
- We need to loosen up, so we're going to think a little more like otters—adding some play to the day
- We need to treat each other more kindly, so we're going to think more like geese—helping each other more

You can pick pretty much any one thing you want to improve, and then find an animal or logo or maxim to focus and reinforce the effort. Many people are visual learners, so having that stuffed animal out or posting pictures or sayings on the refrigerator as a reminder are all easy, inexpensive ways to turn the focus to what's important.

And you need to be deliberate. After figuring what you want to focus on, explain to the group "this is what we're focusing on, and to reinforce it, we're adding this guy [pull out the stuffed animal, or slogan, etc.] to have around our area for the next six months. And let's see how we can work on upping our [fill in the blank] with her help. To be more like a [fill in the blank], we need to focus more on _____ And we'll do it by...

- Adding a step to recheck work before it leaves our area (hawk).
- Sending a short email to our customer asking how we did (border collie).
- Asking our clients if we thought "out of the box" enough for them (fox).
- Reviewing our productivity stats more often (bee).
- Scheduling some fun into our week with a pot luck lunch or ice cream break (otter).
- Creating a rotating buddy system so we can check in with one another more often as people, not just co-workers (goose)."

After a few months you should see some improvement in what you're focusing on; in four-to-six months you should see a definite, now-built-in habit.

This happens because, the words of management guru Peter Drucker, "What gets measured gets done."

Let me repeat that: What Gets Measured Gets Done.

If you truly want to improve an area, a metric, a reputation, you need to figure out what you'll do to correct it, what fun you can add to it to emphasize the point so the change is easier to swallow, and stick to reinforcing that vision for a half year. After that, you can put the saying or stuffed animal aside, in semi-retirement. The totem will still be around, and if you need to bring it back to center focus, for more reinforcement, you can.

You might even consider creating a mascot for your team. There are several "tiger teams" out there, particularly made to take on one special task/problem (A tiger team is a specialized, cross-functional team brought together to solve or investigate a specific problem or critical issue; the term originates from the military and was made famous by NASA which deployed a tiger team during the Apollo 13 mission.) But maybe your group can identify more with a Labrador retriever (loyalty), chameleon (adaptable) or a swan (classy). If you think it might make for a rallying point, consider this idea. There are many directions you can go with a mascot to further brand your team. For a few bucks you can get shirts made up with the logo and wear them on Fridays. You can add it to your stationary and website. And if you work on making that ideal a reality, both outsiders and team members will begin to believe (cue *Pygmalion*).

The smaller group and one-on-one meetings, whether formal or informal, are more opportunities to specifically tailor messages to key sub-groups and individuals.

Ultimately, the more pride you can instill the more you reinforce your message of expectations. The more your team celebrates wins, the greater the team cohesion, and the stronger likelihood of future success.

And, if there are people who aren't buying into it (probably those actively disengaged folks), all the better to make them want to leave!

Now let's drill that down one final level.

You can have Vision or Mission statements for your professional self, just as you have personal professional goals. Examples might include:

1. My career goal is to become a vet working for a large facility in Kansas City. I've always wanted to help dogs and other animals live healthy lives and cure their illnesses. So my Vision is, "To ensure all pets in the KC area live disease-free, healthy lives!"

2. My five-year goal to become the coach of the varsity football team at John Carroll. My Mission is to help young adults learn to play the game at their highest level while building their emotional intelligence and being mindful of God's gifts to us.

3. My Vision is to be someone about whom my children can proudly say, "This is my mom. She has taught me that I need to love and respect both myself and others. She has taught me that taking short cuts make me less valuable to myself and the world, and that growth comes through adversity. And from her I've learned that I am responsible for my happiness and to indulge from time to time is ok to do."

Let's have you sketch out what your Mission and Vision may be right now; start with:

Three things I value: (these could be things such as persistence, inclusion, or sustainability)

1. _____

2. _____

3. _____

Your Vision: a lofty personal goal for 5 to 10 years from now

• _____

Your Mission: how you're going to do it and the purpose (more detailed than your Vision, includes practical day-to-day operations)

• _____

So we have goals and even Missions and Visions for not just organizations, but departments *and* individuals! It's important to regularly reflect on how well you are staying focused on these (set up a tickler reminder on your calendar), and remember that these will need to be updated and changed from time to time, because things like the economy, industry trends, and cultural perspectives change. But you can always do a SWOT and keep pop culture in mind when you design your next great motivator and goals. And remember that while most people do not like change, if they have clarity on why it's happening and see the benefit of what's in it for them, then it's more likely to take root!

Go to the Replay Booth

1. You need to be intentional about things that matter, especially the culture of your area
2. What Gets Measured Gets Done
3. Vision statements are good for individuals as well as groups and organizations

6

ENLIST

The E in "SET" stands for Enlist – each in their role

Leigh Anne: "*Mike, do you remember when we went to that horrible part of town to get your clothes, and I was a little bit scared, but you told me not to worry because you had my back?*"

Michael: "*Uh huh.*"

Leigh Anne: "*And if anyone had tried to get me, you would have stomped them? Tony is your quarterback, when you think of him, you think of me. Are you going to protect the family?*"

Michael: "*Yes ma'am.*"

Leigh Anne: "*Good, go have some fun.*"

That dialog is of course from Sandra Bullock and Quinton Aaron in *The Blind Side* and is a great example of how someone can coach by literally moving players and talking in metaphors they understand to show them how to do their job.

Since you have sold the Vision, it is now time to make sure each person has specifics on how they are to follow through, that they feel personally Enlisted in their position and duties. Whether coaching a tried-and-true vet or a rookie fresh out of college, a good leader makes time to ensure this enlistment. One of the most effective methods is having one-on-one meetings (think of these as more like informal check-ins), at least as often as every two weeks for the rooks and monthly for the vets.

These check-ins are key for a couple of important reasons:

- First, they assure the mission, roles and responsibilities stay clear and in the front of everyone's mind.
- Secondly, you ensure that your employees are getting their number three biggest need fed (see the appendix for the "What Employees Want" table).

As you're doing this, make note of key points from your conversations and put the notes into a file that you can reflect back on, especially when you're doing your (strategic) planning. These notes serve as a refresher of key points and topics from the previous meeting, as well as being very helpful when you have to write up and deliver reviews.

To Enlist someone, you need to get them to understand how their interests and goals tie into the needs and goals for your area. It's human nature to first think "what's in it for me?"

That's why you want to have an intentional, individual talk with each team member as soon as you feel you've put out a clear message about the vision, and you are convinced they're not someone you need to immediately get off the team.

"Now wait…" you might be thinking, "this is beginning to sound like a lot of work. Asking questions of people outside the department before I get in there, configuring who to keep and preparing exit strategies for those we don't want, devising and communicating a vision, and now one-on-ones to enlist them to the vision?! And I'm supposed to do this *when*?!"

And my response is you reap what you sow.

If you don't take these steps in the order they're laid out, your efforts will only go so far, and you will not be as effective down the road as you could and will want to be. It's like a farmer preparing the field before planting. It's like a fisherman grabbing the correct lures for the type of fish they wants to catch. It's like a head coach preparing for the next opponent as soon as the whistle blows to end the game going on right now.

Ben Franklin said, "By failing to prepare, you are preparing to fail." Abe Lincoln said "Give me six hours to chop down a tree and I will spend the first four sharpening the axe." *Paul "Bear" Bryant, famed Alabama coach,* said "It's not the will to win that matters. It's the will to prepare to win that matters." And Homer Simpson said, "Do'h!" a lot because he never prepared. So yeah, the more you want to succeed the more you'll need to do all this. Otherwise people will hear you shouting "do'h!" from your office a lot.

So this tying your vision with their interests and goals is how you will get the group to become a high-performing team.

For example, if you want to start raising productivity:

1. You make productivity a clear part of your vision.

2. You set productivity goals for the team to reach.

3. You communicate the productivity goals (remember, what gets measured get done) every few days with some commentary. That commentary gets done at a team huddle (mid Monday mornings are often good for a team huddle – you set up the week just like the quarterback sets up the play).

4. You put those productivity numbers on a board everyone can see.

5. You add a bee or beaver or Clydesdale logo to help provide a visual and fun reference that gets associated with productivity.

6. And then you reinforce all of it – the productivity vision and goals – in your one-on-ones.

In the one-on-ones, you can go over key productivity and other points that tie directly into the employee's job. You can ask them their thoughts on the why's of patterns and anomalies. You can ask for innovative tweaks or concerns they have for what's down the road. Collect all the feedback and then sort it out, determine the relevance of any of it, and add those valuable insights to your plans for moving forward. Be sure to give employees credit in your team huddles for the insights you use, and the impact they had on the bottom line.

Here's another important suggestion when you are first meeting with your employees and getting to know them: Ask each one how they'd prefer to get an "atta boy" if they do something great. Note everyone wants to be celebrated in the same way. Some people bask in public praise, while others shy away from it, or worse.

One bad-case scenario I can cite occurred when a manager realized that one of her engineers had perfect attendance for over a decade. She put together a surprise celebration with a cake and the whole department in attendance. The engineer, who liked quietly coming to work, taking care of business, and heading home without fanfare was not only surprised but embarrassed. She did not like the attention focused solely on her.

Worse yet, from that point on the engineer made sure to occasionally take days off just so she never again would have perfect attendance over a long period—the opposite of what the public celebration was meant to encourage.

It is vital to know what the boundaries of your people are. Everyone's different, so expect slightly different boundaries. Introverts may be less likely to want attention, such as in the case above.

One thing I like to practice when I meet a new member of our team is to ask them how they would like to be rewarded or recognized for a job well done, and make note of that. The fact that you make it personalized to their comfort level is a good way to grow the connection with them, and as a by-product to better connect them with the organization.

Go to the Replay Booth

1. Tie your vision with their interests and goals
2. A weekly team huddle creates a stronger sense of team and wider understanding of what's going on
3. Treat your people the way they want to be treated

7

TRAIN

The T in "SET" stands for Train—team members on the basics as well as to their interests

---

General Barnicke: "Are you telling me that you men finished your training on your own?"

John Winger: "That's the fact, Jack!"

Soldiers: "That's the fact, Jack!"

—ROBERT WILKE, BILL MURRAY, ET AL;
STRIPES, 1981

Training Industry Quarterly pointed out that training camps traditionally start in March for college teams and in July for the NFL, 7 months and 6 weeks respectively before they start playing regular season games. How nice would it be if you actually had that much time to prepare a new hire before they actually started working for you? That would be pretty sweet, considering it typically takes several weeks for a person to feel comfortable in the job, and up to a year or more before they can be considered fully productive. And few of us are likely to get a self-motivated, self-training team such as General Barnicke in our quote above.

One of my mentors, Jay, loved to tell the story of an enlightened GM of a large employer who, when considering buying a training program, was asked by a production manager, "What happens if we train our employees and they then leave us?" The GM, not missing a beat, replied, "What happens if we <u>don't</u> train our employees and they <u>don't</u> leave us???" Jay's point obviously being that if you don't try to get better, you won't—and you'll suffer the consequences of stagnation.

One of the things that disheartens me is how little time most organizations put into training their employees. If you want to grow your revenues you're going to have to get better. And, yes, there are a wide variety of methods you can use to do that. For instance, "getting better" questions can include:

Do you double down on your biggest loss leader?

Do you double down on your best cost-profit ratio?

Do you expand into a direct or indirect product or service?

Regardless of what you decide to do, you're probably going to have to teach your employees how to improve. Whether that's on a mechanical process, an efficiency improvement, or how to better manage people and situations, you've going to have to INVEST TIME.

Sure, if you invest time on training, then your immediate short-term opportunity cost is going to be lower production. This is where many people fail to see the magic.

Please recognize that if you never invest the time to train your people, they will never get better (except for those who *may* slowly learn through osmosis from watching others). If in doing your job as a leader you don't assure that your employees are given opportunities to learn, they won't learn. And your organization will suffer in the long run, resulting in slower growth.

You have a choice. You can either slow down production/service that will show up on the daily or weekly report to get better gains on your monthly and annual report, or you can choose to remain flat with token growth at the end of the year.

HR expert Susan Heathfield points out that one byproduct of training is employee loyalty (read: Retention! BAM! Lower costs in turnover. Remember, turnover costs are typically much higher than training costs).

Here's a brief example of the cost differential:

Training 5 people who make $20/hour for one day:

> 5 people x $20 x 8 hours = $800 labor cost

> Multiply that by whatever benefits you give them (we'll say +25%) = $200

> Add in whatever cost for materials and (if need be) an outside trainer; say another $800

> Lost labor and added cost for the day = $1,800

Compared that to the cost of turnover for 1 employee who makes $20/hour:

> Cost of Turnover = (Cost of Hiring + Cost of Onboarding and Training + Severance/Unemployment + Loss in Productivity).

> HR studies show that it costs employers about one-third of a worker's annual salary to hire a replacement if that worker leaves. So, $20 x 2080 hours/year divided by 33% = $13,866.

> Add in your time and frustration for counseling the employee because their performance is not where it needs to be.

I'd tell you to do the math, but I just did it for us.

$$13,866 > 1,800$$

You're spending a lot more money for NOT training than if you provided the training.

Add to that the emotional lift your production gets if you are actively engaged with your workers. You're getting that "I like working here" bump that an actively engaged employee brings.

There are a few cases when this dream can actually be pulled off. Depending on the job and your local or state government, there are programs through job prep agencies that will pay for training in part or in whole. You definitely want to look into this for your area!

One of my clients was a young manager of an auto rental shop for a huge auto dealer. A career employee of 16 years, she had never been given any formal training and was struggling to manage her growing department. Up to that point she had gotten by on reading a few management books and watching YouTube videos. She knew things weren't right but didn't know how to fix them, and her boss offered no guidance but for a recent edict to "make things work better" after complaints began to rise. After our first meeting it was clear that while she still liked the company she felt like an island with little support.

Together we were able to help her realize that this was actually a great opportunity to create new expectations of behavioral standards and a climate of support. We talked about everything from the physical look and layout of the office, to training on customer service and organizing, to using Myers Briggs Type Indicator and DiSC personality test for personal insights, and implementing methods to collect customer and employee feedback. We even discussed creating a mascot to reinforce her team's identity.

She shared this with her assistant manager and boss. The assistant manager loved it, and immediately began creating ways to incorporate these ideas. Unfortunately the manager's boss didn't agree, saying it would be too costly in time and money, so it went nowhere. Less than a year later both the manager and assistant manager had left, and this ridiculously wealthy dealership spent more money replacing them than if they had moved ahead with what was beginning to energize the department.

Training is even more important today because of the millions of Gen Z'ers who are entering the workforce. They and the Millennials are easily the most educated generations ever, in a large part because they see the value of knowledge and actually like to learn. In fact, they are much more likely to leave an organization if they feel they are not learning (especially something that does not interest them). And of course growth opportunities are another factor that contributes to employee satisfaction!

Go to the Replay Booth

1. If you don't try to get better, you won't
2. Opportunity costs rarely outweigh the cost of well-run training programs
3. What happens if you don't train your employees and they don't leave?

Reviewing SET

Selling the vision of your organization is key. Most people are willing to be led, but they need to believe in the leader and his/her vision. Is it clear to them? Do they believe it's achievable? Do they hear you talk about your vision periodically, and discuss how each of them tie into it?

If you can achieve this, then you can easily **Enlist** them into their role, get them to take calculated risks (because now they aren't afraid to), and echo your vision to others.

One of the things you owe all of your employees is ensuring they have the skills to achieve what you ask of them—and that means **Training** them. It has to be relevant; they have to see the connection to their work. And as they learn and become competent at one skill, you need to then train them on the next, and the next, and the next. In time you'll see who your rising stars are, and get everyone placed where they will be successful AND like what they do. And that will motivate the entire team.

Can you smell the victory in the air?!

PART THREE

LISTEN

The Stance and Pick the Right Posture

— 8 —

LISTEN

The L in "LEAD" stands for Listen—to what they want (passions)

"Help me... help you. Help me help you!"

— TOM CRUISE AS JERRY MAGUIRE,
JERRY MAGUIRE, (1996)

In the film *Jerry Maguire*, the scene with this quote has sports agent Jerry pleading with his client Rod Tidwell for an opportunity to listen to his message, his side of the story. They were two guys aiming for the same thing, but with different ideas on how to get it accomplished.

Perhaps it is in training camp when you see Listening in its most active state. Coaches are imparting knowledge it is vital to the team's success. If the players don't listen and don't get it, they don't make the team. When the games begin you see it in an even more intentional way. As quarterbacks are relaying the play in the huddle to their 10 teammates, they are often doing so in a pressure cooker. The play clock is rolling and they need to get the team to the line. The quarterback then needs to assess if what they see from the defensive alignment will work, or if they need to audible to another play. If you watch closely when that happens you will see teammates checking with one another to make sure they have the message correct. It's vital because if any one of those

10 teammates doesn't correctly listen they could blow the play and the team loses yardage.

It's all about communication. That old adage about having two ears and one mouth exists for a reason, because the majority of communication should be two words: you listening.

I'm a huge proponent of the old MBWA concept—Management By Walking Around. I also like the show *Undercover Boss*, and *A Christmas Carol* (or Bill Murray's movie *Scrooged* to be exact). Why? Because they are all about managers who reconnect with their people. These are men and women who know (or re-learn) that their time is best spent with employees who do the work necessary for the organization to success-fully move on to tomorrow.

Why is MBWA so vital? Because NOTHING is better than face-to-face meetings. A famous study that was the basis for the book *Silent Messages* reported that only 7% of a message's meaning is communicated through spoken word, while 38% is through your tone of voice and 55% is through body language. And also because employees respond better when they see their leader walking around interacting with them as opposed to being in a far off office and never seeing them.

One of the tools I sometimes use to help professionals get a better understanding of how to communicate is the Johari Window. The name sounds impressive until you learn it was created by two guys, Joe and Harry. Seriously. But these two did create a sensible technique for under-standing how and why people understand and communicate knowledge.

Essentially it uses four quadrants or (window) panes to identify what is known by you and others, to a point:

1. You know, others do not know about you (Hidden)
2. Others know, you do not realize about yourself (Blind)
3. Everyone knows (Open)
4. No one knows (Unknown)

The goal is to increase the Open, and decrease the others. Providing 360° feedback (input from everyone in the work group, including the frontline employees) helps a lot to widen the Open pane, but it requires the trust to listen.

With the growth of remote working and teleworking, the stakes have become even greater. Not only do you have to drive 75 yards to score now, but you have to do it without one of the resources that was always there—the quick walk down the hall. That growing challenge encompasses managing goals and outcomes and not tasks, managing results versus activity, and teaching people to coach themselves. You'll need to cover how often, when, and how you'll talk. This is vital because when you break down how people communicate, 93% of it is through body language and tone; only 7% is through the actual words you use!

One way to see how you're currently doing is by asking yourself (and trusted peers who know you well) these questions, rating yourself 1—5 on:

- How strong the relationship is
- How often you communicate to individuals
- The opportunity you give yourself to show respect and appreciation, and give feedback
- How often your team gets together
- The sense of "a team" that your group has developed

If your average is 3 or lower, you have some work to do!

Back in the day when I headed the HR office at a large distribution center, I would regularly grab a Polaroid camera and go out on the floor and just start snapping pictures of people. They loved it because it was an immediate spirit lifter. No matter how bad a day they were having they loved grabbing their friends, smiling for the birdie, and getting an immediate keep-sake they could take home or tack up in their area. And...another positive was they got to know me better, so it wasn't necessarily a bad thing when they saw the guy from HR suddenly show up. And they began to feel better about coming into the HR suite for help and participating in building events.

Going back to those initial conversations with HR, trusted partners, and clients you'll have when you're first hired, it is time to learn first-hand from the people on your team what they want and how they see things. The best way to initiate this process is to use the exercise in the back of this book, New Leader Onboarding. That will immediately help break the ice and speed up the "get to know you" process.

This is because there are four steps in how a team forms: Forming, Storming, Norming, and Performing. By using this Onboarding exercise you are taking a hack saw to the first (Forming) stage. Like Buffalo quarterback Jim Kelly chopping up a defense to score a last-second touchdown, in using this exercise you are getting through the Forming stage far more quickly. You can use the feedback from the Onboarding exercise for talking points when you meet individually with each person the first week that you are there.

Yes - you need to meet with every direct report on your team the first week you are there. And you need to make sure that your boss understands that. Even if you are walking into a firestorm business-wise, you need to make sure that you are getting information by meeting with your people immediately upon your arrival.

If this means you have to work extra hours your first week, so be it. Being the right person for this job means you will take the necessary steps to make sure it's done, and done well. And if you do happen to step into a firestorm, remember the adage that being calm breeds calm, panic breeds panic, and stupid breeds stupid.

At the end of your New Leader Onboarding exercise you want to let your team know that you plan to meet with each of them individually later that week for up to 30 minutes, and that they should be prepared to answer these two questions:

1. "What we really need is _____", and

2. "What would be really cool is _____."

If someone has a key personal concern they want to discuss with you, the New Leader Onboarding exercise is not the time or place. There is work to do and if it's an HR/personal issue, they should go to HR.

To illustrate this investment, let's say you have six employees in your Inbound Department. By taking 30 minutes out of each day to meet individually with each of them that first week (preferably not in your office area so you can make it seem less formal and more conversational), and doubling up on Wednesday, by the end of the week you will have learned what got them to the position they are in.

To reinforce your learnings, immediately after each meeting use a Post It note to write down all the things you discovered the two of you have in common. Keep that on the inside cover of the personnel file you have for them. That way you can easily access and remember what you have in common, until they finally become part of the natural flow of conversation.

In those first-week individual meetings you want to go over what was covered in the Onboarding exercise and ask them what they got out of it and what their concerns are.

As you are listening to them, make sure you are taking notes and are fully engaged. If they say something that brings a question to your mind, ask them to stop for a moment, get the question down, and then let them continue from where you stopped them. Then go back to your questions. You don't want to go down the rabbit hole when they could be telling you some pertinent information that you would miss while in that rabbit hole.

Focus your conversation first to learn more about them personally and their professional career path, then around their answers to the two questions above. Find out where they came from all the way from the beginning and you will perhaps find some interesting stories as to why people are who and where they are now. And spend several quality minutes talking about how they feel about their job. Ask how they were scored on their last review and any comments they have about it. Ask them, "What do you want to be when you grow up?" Feel free to use those words; it will take make things a tad lighter.

And remember to ask them for their answer those two questions:

1. "What we really need is _____", and

2. "What would be really cool is _____."

It's vital to walk away knowing what you have in common with each person. Because it doesn't matter how *little* you have in common with them—you could be the opposite gender, race, age, political affiliation, and a lot more. The point you want to show is that everyone has something in common with everyone on the face of this earth. Your job is to find multiple commonalities you share with each of them, so that you have some common points to discuss and build a relationship from. Finding and then coming from this common ground can help reinforce the organization's core principles, Mission, and Vision.

After a while, when you are beyond your area just keeping up and are now beginning to see how you can improve your area's systems and processes, the answer to the second question, "What would be really cool is _____" is what will lead you to innovate to take your area to the next level of performance.

Even after holding the Onboarding exercise and the initial week 30-minute individual meetings, managers ought to have mini conversations with all their workers weekly. It doesn't matter if it's in a warehouse, on a worksite, or in the office.

Earlier I said that the one thing people like to talk most about is themselves. (Hey, even I admit that is kinda why I wrote this book.) So by tapping into that human desire, you can easily find out what it is that really stokes your employees. Again, this all comes back to being intentional about what you do. It means that you have to specifically take time to figure out what makes your people tick. In the end this will be huge win for you.

One of the happiest moments of my career was when I was able to gift something very meaningful to a great employee who kicked ass on a huge project. Our Safety Manager, Leonard, had worked for months on an important program that touched every point on the distribution system. When he wrapped up, I asked our GM for permission to get him a unique and impactful gift.

Leonard was traveling to the LA area to conclude the program. I knew from our regular chats that he was a huge Lakers fan. Fortunately, it was basketball season and the Lakers were in town during his visit, so we got him a seat on the floor at a game. He was completely speechless when we presented it to him. From the time he came back he wouldn't stop talking about it. As you can imagine, he was even more invested in his job after that!

Without going in depth on using personality tests, I recommend that if you have Myers Briggs or DiSC profiles on your employees that you review and use the results to plan *how* to talk with each individual. If you don't, at least first consider how each person might prefer to be communicated to. In Myers Briggs talk, introverts should be approached differently than extroverts (start with an email versus barging into their office). In DiSC talk, you approach a D much differently (directly) than an I (inspirationally) if you want a positive interaction. And generationally speaking, Boomers are going to respond differently than Millennials! Just bare that in mind so you can add to your impact.

Go to the Replay Booth

1. Talk with everyone on your team individually the very first week you are there

2. Ask them how they prefer to communicate, and what their career inspirations are

3. Together discuss how you could try to tie those personal aspirations in with the vision and goals of the company/department

CONTRIBUTOR ADDENDUM:

Listen

BY MARQUES OGDEN, JACKSONVILLE JAGUARS

(see page 120 for Marques' bio and contact information)

In 2003 I was a rookie with the Jacksonville Jaguars, and our head coach was Jack Del Rio. Jack was a phenomenal football player, who was in his rookie year as a Head Coach in the National Football League in 2003. Right out of the gate, Jack earned the respect of all of his players. He was honest, fair, tough, supportive, nurturing, and he was by far one of the most reliable coaches I ever had the pleasure of playing for.

I'll never forget in 2003, he spoke to all of us rookies individually and told us all about how much of a honor it was to be drafted by the Jacksonville Jaguars, along with some ground rules for playing on his team.

Top 3 rules were:

1. Respect each other
2. Respect people in the community
3. Never ever be late

These rules I felt were pretty normal, and they were very easy and simplistic to process and follow. Another thing that Jack told us all individually, and as a team unit was that "we are all our own CEOs." What Jack meant by that was, in life you are the boss and commander of your own destiny. This statement really made a huge positive impact on me, as Jack was really telling us that "we are our own brand!" Yes, we worked for the Jacksonville Jaguars, yes we worked for the National Football League, but most importantly we WORKED FOR OURSELVES... on the football field, off the football field, in the community, talking to the media; everything we did was a reflection of our own personal brands! That saying has stuck with me ever since, and will until the day I'm no longer on this earth.

During our individual incoming talks with the Jaguars, I'll never forget when Jack asked "Marques, what type of coaching style do you respond best to?"

I remember I had this look of bewilderment on my face, and I asked him "Coach, what do you mean?"

He said "Marques, what kind of coaching style do you respond best to? That doesn't mean you will be coached that way of course, but I just want to know what type of communication you respond best to!" That day I realized for the first time, how much of a business the NFL really was.

Any good boss is going to want to know what kind of communication style their employees respond best to, this way they can get the best out of those employees. Also, a great leader knows that you have to talk to different members of your team in different ways. Having "a universal language" for everyone that you serve as a leader is not the trait of a great leader. So I'll always appreciate Jack making me see and understand the business side of the NFL.

During that talk, Jack asked me the most profound question in my professional career up to that point... "Marques, what are your personal goals for being here with the Jaguars in the NFL?"

I remember looking at Jack and saying "Coach, I want to make the team, and be a contributor as quickly as I can and I'll do whatever it takes to get there!"

Coach Del Rio then said to me "Ok Marques, that's your goal, now let me tell you the goals of The Jaguars:

1. Goal #1 Be the best team in the NFL
2. Goal #2 Have a strong and positive relationship with the Jaguar fan community

3. Goal #3 Have a strong, healthy team locker room culture

His next statement to me was the following "Marques, how can your personal goal of making the team, align with any or all of the Jaguar goals?"

Answering that question for Jack was one of the most positive, intense filled moments of my life! I was full of energy, my blood was pumping through my veins, and I literally was so excited to hit the field after I told him how my goals would align with the Jaguars goals!

That 30 minute conversation with Jack Del Rio truly set the tone for me as a professional athlete in the NFL. In that time with him I saw how much he cared for me as a person, by the way he engaged me. I saw how much he cared by the way he tried to find my communication style. But most of all I saw how he worked hard to align my goals and values with those of the Jacksonville Jaguars, which was one of the most impactful moments of my life.

In life, we have to learn how to communicate with our team. What makes them tick? What's their pattern recognition? What are their long-term/short-term goals. Finding all this information out and learning how to TRULY LISTEN as a leader, gives you the best chance to succeed!

Humor is a gift bestowed by the gods. If you have a good sense of it, you should most certainly use it to the best of your ability. I have found using a little levity can make a huge difference in building and maintaining relationships as well as help calm rough episodes. If you don't have a strong one, believe it or not it is a skill you can learn and apply in the workplace. There are actual classes and several good books (*Humor That Works*, for one) on developing your sense of humor and learning how to apply it.

For example, one effective use of humor I found as a young dad was when I was leaving work to call my kids at the house. Without saying it was me, I would say, "Hey, I just saw your dad leave work, so he'll be home in about 30 minutes. So if the house is a mess or you haven't started your homework, you may want to fix that, 'cause he'd probably not be happy if that's that case!" They'd laugh and say, "Ok, thanks for the heads up!" In essence I was giving them a humorous warning that I was headed home, so get your act together so I won't be mad!

The same concept is applicable at work. When you're talking about a deadline you could go on about how ugly the boss (you) can get when deadlines are missed. It is just a light hearted way to reinforce expectations and show more of your human side.

You don't have to use these exact tactics: You should make the humor your own, just as different comics use their own voice and experiences when describing the same situation. Just be sure to know your boundaries so you aren't sent down to HR like Michael Scott of *The Office* (or the infamous Jerry Richardson, former owner of the Carolina Panthers).

9

EMPOWER

The E in LEAD stands for Empower

"The way it works is, you do the thing you're scared shitless of, and you get the courage after you do it, not before you do it."

— GEORGE CLOONEY AS ARCHIE GATES, *THREE KINGS* (1999)

Now that you have listened to your employees (and hopefully they have listened to you), you need to help empower them to achieve what it is they are responsible for. This might be the most difficult step for a couple of reasons. First off, you have to let go of the reins. Second, they need to be comfortable taking the reins. The only way this happens is by developing trust between the two of you, which is not always easy work.

One of the best ways to grow trust is to learn what the employees see as obstacles in their way to getting their job done, and helping them devise plans to get rid of those obstacles. Empowering them to do this makes them more confident and encourages them to take bigger steps.

Getting rid of obstacles may be natural for some people, difficult for others. Many people are happy to do just what they are doing, and no more. If that is their sincere desire, you need to make sure that they are aware of the consequences of their decision and subsequent inaction, that they may ultimately be pigeon-holed with little growth while others pass them by. This may be perfectly fine with them. Perhaps they have other things in their lives they would prefer to devote time and focus to, or maybe they just don't want to work any harder.

If they are effective and efficient in a position, there is no reason to move them on. In fact, folks like this can make wonderful stanchions that you can build around. They can prove to be a solid and enduring piece to your team, that plug that is always there for you to count on. They'll never be a superstar, but as long as they are good at what they're doing and the workflow process needs them, you should encourage them to keep doing as they are.

Relative to the NFL, think of it as how general managers work within the salary cap. After paying the superstars they feel they need to keep, it becomes crucial to find players who can reasonably fill out the other roles. They show up, they perform, and hopefully they didn't drive the coaches and fans too crazy with missed assignments.

The good news is you aren't necessarily dealing with a hard cap and/or the crazy-rich contracts that limit NFL general managers.

As your employees are developing their plans for attaining their annual goal, you should encourage them to figure out how to improve performance or surpass the goal. Encourage them to get creative. Many organizations deter creativity, but the greatest gains are usually made because someone was inquisitive enough to try something new or to reach beyond the norm.

Go back to the example in the Negotiate section when I started training one of our HR clerks on how to do unemployment claim investigations. The light in her eyes went from hum drum to being really excited. She loved researching why the person left and preparing for their arguments in the hearing and she was damn good at it. In a very short period, she went from being disengaged to engaged with her work. She started asking for more to do and began seeing a career path in her future.

For those who are looking for greater empowerment, it is easy to get them to do so by focusing on whatever annual goals they have. Most everybody has some sort of a list of annual goals, but too often their supervisor does not work with them to figure out a plan on how to get it done. To the extent of the employee's experience, you should help them create a plan to do so.

A rookie is going to need a lot more hands-on attention than a seasoned vet. That is not to say that you should micro-manage! In fact, you should NEVER micro-manage. There is never a good time or reason to micro-manage!

This is so important I'll repeat it again: there is never a good time or reason to micro-manage.

(OK, I will grant you that ordering everyone out of building when it is on fire might be viewed as micro-managing. I guess you could let each employee make his or her own decision about when to leave. So, yes, a true life-threatening emergency might be the exception to the rule.)

When an employee or team is micro-managed stressors are created, innovation evaporates, and all of the energy is sapped out of the group. They'll begin feeling that they're being called for offsides or a false start on back-to-back plays, and perpetually looking at third and 25. That's no fun. That's when players start looking for other places to play, and employees look to jump ship.

Think of a time when you worked for a micro-manager - we all have, right? Was it fun? Of course not. Typically, people micro-manage when they are insecure. They are grasping at whatever power they have, and will make sure that you know who has the power. These managers have bad reputations and very unhappy workers. When you are the general manager of the team, these micro-managers are the people you need to get off of your team.

One of the golden rules in HR is to look for your organization's highest turnover areas. That's where you'll typically find your worst supervisors, who are probably micromanaging a bunch of very sad, frustrated people who are considering jumping ship.

Another way to empower is to educate or train your employees. There is always someone out there ready, willing, and able to instruct your employees on anything from using QuickBooks to providing better customer service. And who doesn't like to make their job easier?!

Again, when compared with the cost of turnover or not improving, the price to pay for an expert to train your employees is quite often far less than not doing so. The key to educating employees is to make sure that they grasp it and then apply it. Once your employee has completed a training program (whether it was online or off at a conference), have them give a short presentation on what they learned. It could be anything from a 2-minute update in a team huddle meeting to a 15 minute, five-slide PowerPoint.

This is another great opportunity for employees to grow. Public speaking is one of the scariest things to humans; the vast majority of people would rather eat bugs or have surgery than give a public presentation. Folks who are painfully shy will avoid this at all costs. It's not that you should force them to do this, but give them the opportunity to bolster their confidence by making a presentation, or at least reporting back.

Pay for them to join Toast Masters, one of the best, most cost-effective training experiences around. That's because if you ever really want to truly learn something, you need to teach it. The ultimate goal is to reinforce what they've learned. And the more they practice something they have just learned, the better they will be at it. Practice, practice, practice brings perfection. If they put their new learnings to repetitive use, it will become habit and your employees will become more effective, efficient, and valuable.

It's not easy to get all the pieces to fall together just right, but as you get close to perfecting the system, having the right talent happily doing their thing with people they like being around, you'll begin to see magic happen. The synergy, the combined effect that is greater than the sum of their separate effects, is how a successful team blossoms. Employees get excited and proud that their efforts are running smoothly, setting new record KPIs, and that they are growing their professional skills. It's almost like watching the exuberance of players when they realize all that listening and practicing has paid off. They're leaping into each other after TD's, slapping each other on the shoulder pads and smiling from ear to ear on the sideline.

Daniel Pink, one of my favorite management gurus to follow, wrote about three key components of intrinsic motivation: autonomy, mastery, and purpose. Pink basically states that being able to control what you do enhances innovation; while the drive for mastery promotes higher productivity and effectiveness; and tying personal goals with professional goals creates a sense of purpose that will also drive improved outcomes. Give team members the chance to spend 10 percent of their working time on a company-focused project of their own choice, something that will either improve efficiencies, revenue, or cut costs. You'll be surprised what cool concepts they develop!

When you're successful, your area will become a high-quality, experienced team. Who doesn't love watching a team that's really got their game down? And the public will pay for that quality.

One of my favorite work fables is about a guy who had his dead auto towed to a shop to get fixed. The mechanic took all of 10 minutes to diagnose and fix the car (poke a hole in a valve), yet charged him $100. The guy was upset. "What?! A hundred dollars for poking a hole in the car to fix it?!"

The mechanic said "No, poking hole was only $3. Knowing where to poke the hole from 20 years of experience, that was $97."

Cheeky, but you can't argue with getting what you pay for.

Go to the Replay Booth

1. Handing over power to your people requires trust on both sides, but you won't grow as a leader or team if you don't do it
2. Success breeds synergy
3. NEVER micro-manage

CONTRIBUTOR ADDENDUM

Empower

BY DOUG PLANK, CHICAGO BEARS

(see page 121 for Doug's bio and contact information)

Empower them. Everyone wants power. It can be in a society or it can be in a family or even on a sports team. The ability to make decisions during your life or even a game can determine the success or failure of your cause.

Most sports decisions are made by the coaches in a press box or on the field. Family decisions are made by the parents. What about allowing everyone to make decisions? If you can educate people to make educated decisions, they feel much better about those decisions. This is called empowerment. People want to have control over their decisions and actions. By empowering people you build confidence and trust into their actions. This is true in all phases of life. It's true for families, businesses, and sports teams.

In 1985, the Chicago Bears defensive coordinator Buddy Ryan empowered his defense by creating the "46" Defense, allowing them to make choices about pass coverages and pass rush for each play. Each week Buddy Ryan put together a game plan of defensive alignments and coverages for passes and runs that the opponents ran in the last three games. By using probabilities, he matched choices of defensive options for each down and distance and the football location on the field. This resulted in every decision being made by a player on the field during the game just before the ball was snapped.

The Chicago Bears defense developed incredible energy and effort by allowing the players to make decisions and not the coaches. The players would line up and gather energy from each other before the snap. Each player knew exactly what he was to do because he was just given that information by the middle linebacker. By empowering the defense, the Chicago Bears defense played at a level that was never seen in the National Football League. They not only executed the defense but they had incredible enthusiasm during the game. This was a result of being empowered. They made every decision. The players would sacrifice for each other because they were given total freedom to choose and execute whatever defense they wanted.

By empowering players, you gave them the confidence about making decisions for the Chicago Bears defense. The concept was so successful that it led the NFL in defensive statistics and also a Super Bowl win. By empowering the players, it provided great dividends for the Chicago Bears organization.

10

ADVOCATE

The A in "LEAD" stands for Advocate

"My boy is wicked sma(r)t!"

— CASEY AFFLECK AS MORGAN,
GOOD WILL HUNTING (1997)

At this point, you have your team on the road to success. Sir Richard Branson claims if leaders take care of their employees, the employees will take care of everything else. Former Pittsburgh coach Bill Cowher (a.k.a. The Chin) said "when you're successful, it's easier to expect success". At this point you should have a team that can run on their own. Your people understand the Vision, Mission, and KPIs and are (getting) comfortable going out on their own, bolstered by thoroughly understanding their role, and having a degree of autonomy in how they do their job. As Casey puts it in the quote above, you can now brag that your team is "wicked sma(r)t"! (For those who haven't seen the movie, it's based in Massachusetts, hence the dropped "r". For perhaps the funniest football themed example of this accent, Google *Saturday Night Live's* February 2018 skit right before the Eagles/Pats Super Bowl.)

No doubt your peers and others will have noticed a difference in how your team is acting and performing, from the uptick in customer service as well as the comments they hear about how you are on a positive trajectory. There's an actual buzz of happiness from your department. You're transforming the not-engaged into the engaged.

What your folks need at this point is an advocate, someone who will essentially market them to the rest of the organization and their clients. You, having a good reputation and being their boss, are in the perfect position to do this.

Essentially, you should now be spreading the word to anyone and everyone about how good your team has become and how your KPIs are looking better and better. Publicly give praise and credit. I'd highly recommend that you ID one or two examples for each of your employees, stories that you can share with the people you talk to and the people they work with. Think of this as keeping the motor oiled.

For example, if Rich is suddenly getting new clients at a much faster rate, or Carol is teaching her team how to do partner inspections and is decreasing mistakes, or your overall productivity is up by 3.5%, these are things that you want to announce. No one is going to cheer for you harder than you will, no one knows your inside workings as well as you do. You need to be the one out front advocating for your folks.

Advocacy also means that you are getting other people to reconsider past performance and encouraging them to have greater faith, take larger chances, and reset the relationship with your people. For example, if there has been a forever long lukewarm relationship between Todd in your area and Accounts Receivable, it might be a good idea for you, Todd, and the AR manager to get together for 30 minutes to review Todd's new skills and accomplishments. You want to do this in a more-or-less casual way, perhaps inviting the AR manager to your area so they can see and hear the positive buzz for themselves. Hopefully you can do some homework and find what similarities or interests Todd and the AR manager share and start the conversation on that track. Remember, the more you have in common with someone, the more likely they are to pay attention to and like you.

And this needs to go beyond one-on-one meetings between your people and the clients they serve.

One of the best moves I've ever seen is when the manager of Department A does a guest visit to Departments B, C, and D during one of each of their regular meetings and spends 10 to 15 minutes giving an update on the positive changes happening in Department A.

Then Manager A follows up by asking how together they might improve interactions between the departments.

This is a major, major attention grabber. Think of it! Here's an outsider coming in to share information and extending their hand in hopes of creating an even better relationship and process between the two departments. It all takes less than 30 minutes if things go well. And afterwards, if it makes sense for your employees to meet with employees from the other department(s) to iron out specific processes, all the better.

Another interesting and impactful move we did at the distribution center was take our pickers and packers to visit the stores, and assist in stocking shelves. And it wasn't just the highest performers who went: Anyone could and did go. It gave both the DC and the store employees a much better idea of how their work tied together, as well as provided a change of pace AND strengthened understanding and appreciation between two groups that typically never met. Productivity went up, damages went down, and they shared their experiences with teammates around the lunch table. It was very powerful.

Advocacy for your mature group of employees is vital to long-term success and positive reputation building. Once you know you have something to be proud of, you need to go brag about it. Pull outsiders into your areas that they wouldn't normally see, whether they are dotted line, in-house clients, or in some other part of the chain. Because if you don't advocate, no one will!

Go to the Replay Booth

1. If you don't call attention to your wins, not many people will know about them.
2. Visit other areas in your organization to get the word out on your successes, and invite their members to team with yours on ironing out processes between them
3. Your people will hear that you're out bragging on them. Can you imagine how good that will make them feel?

— 11 —

DEVELOP

The D in "LEAD" stands for Develop – them as a mentor, and into becoming a mentor

"Wax on, wax off."

—PAT MORITA AS MR. MIYAGI,
THE KARATE KID (1984)

At this point the thing you should focus on is keeping your now-motivated and high functioning team going. You have some wins and your team is gaining a better reputation. It doesn't happen overnight, and the worse your reputation was before, the longer it may ultimately take to turn it around. But in those unfortunate cases, the worse the reputation, the more that a positive change will be noted. Some people may notice a team who improves from a 6-11 record one year to a 9-8 record the next (hey, it's a winning team now!), but they'll really notice a 4-13 team jumping to an 8-9 team. Might not be quite winning just yet, but you don't suck anymore!

Mentoring on the football field is sometimes a head scratcher. Some guys are cool with helping their successor, others aren't. When Joe Flacco went from Baltimore to Denver, second round draft pick Drew Lock was already waiting there on the Bronco's depth chart. "I hope he does develop" Flacco commented, but then added "I don't look at that as my job."

Conversely, I remember watching a game where former Alabama great Tua Tagovailoa was in the midst of leading the Miami Dolphins on a playoff run, having replaced journeyman superstar Ryan Fitzpatrick midway through the season. In that important late-season game against the Las Vegas Raiders, coach Brian Flores pulled the struggling Tagovalioa for Fitzpatrick, who led the Dolphins to a dramatic comeback win. During the game and for the rest of the season, the two quarterbacks continued to talk and show their support for one another, as was pointed out with some marvel by the game's announcers. "They call him 'Fitzmagic' for a reason," Tagovailoa noted afterwards.

Swallowing your pride and making room in the spotlight for someone else ain't easy, Yet, for those who shift their point of view from "I can help by giving my best" to "I can have a greater influence by training someone with a lot of promise," the impact on both the organization and the new mentor is an undeniably good one.

Perhaps it's harder in sports than in business, but anywhere it's important to have a culture of mentoring to develop talent. Formal mentoring programs are huge in that they bolster retention, account-ability, institutional knowledge, and job satisfaction, to name a few vital points.

You should be the cheerleader not only for your individual team mem-bers, but for the group overall. In meetings you should be touting your team wins and pointing out the improvements over past performance. This will ensure others are aware of your progress and wins. Your role has really become that of a mentor, and you should encourage them as intrapreneurs. That means that people who are (re)inventing things within your area are running it as if it were their own company.

There are fewer things more exhilarating than being a small business owner. And the fertile ground allows them to act as one even though they are in the protective arms of the larger company. As a mentor you are focusing less on managing them and more on acting as an advisor whom they can go to as needed. They know what to do day-by-day, and even week-by-week. Your role is to make sure that they focus on their overarching goals and assist as they come up with unique issues and or problems.

When you revisit your employees and what they listed long ago as their goals and interests, help them compare what those choices were then to where they are now, identify how far they have come, and what else they need to do to reach that goal. It's possible that they have already reached it, or that goal has changed.

In either case, you need to reevaluate how and or why that happened, and what new goal should be in its place. It's possible they have already figured that out, but it's always nice to have a more experienced set of eyes review it and help fine-tune it.

Getting back to my earlier mention of the Johari Window in the Listen chapter; when you have gotten to the point where there is a high degree of trust in your team, using methods such as 360-degree feedback will provide a platform where others can make suggestions for improvement without fear of seeming like it's nitpicking, piling on, or being hurtful. Growth comes from facing adversity, and honest feedback given in a caring way is perhaps the best and safest way to get that next score.

Further development opportunities include setting your people up with others who may know more than you about a particular topic or have a different style and approach that you still like. Making those connections for your employees only helps further develop them.

By looking at your Rolodex (er, contact database), LinkedIn network, or just names in your email address book, find three to five people who may be able to offer new takes on your employee's interests and goals. Offer your employee an introduction and let them take it from there. Circle back a few weeks later to make sure they have connected and, if they haven't, remind them that they are making you look bad as well as themselves if they aren't following up.

From those three to five people your employee will determine who they best connect with and develop a relationship there that will help them grow.

The concept is simple: Spread out a small variety of options and let them choose which path to take. As the initiator, you know that any of these new connections would be a good one, and you are letting them tailor the experience to how they would like it. In giving them that freedom you increase the chance for their success.

Understand that as a mentor the formal aspects of the relationship probably shouldn't last more than about 6 months. If you are touching base with a mentee, then you should be checking in at least bi-weekly and having a thorough discussion to catch up at least monthly. But after about six months you will have most likely run the full course of whatever formal tutoring you can offer and then it will be time for them to move on to another and for you to pick up a new mentee.

At this point you have got your team pretty well set. Or at least you have several people set, and are still working on the others. But for those who have gotten into your system and are beginning to really perform, they obviously don't need as much of a hands-on approach as when you first came in and were selling your plan.

So how do you deal with a more mature workforce? Typically, the best way is to continue to check in on them periodically. Remember: Regardless of how long employees have been in the organization and how experienced they are, they still have a high need to feel appreciated, included, and feel that you give a darn about them. That flows best from regular check-ins.

You can step up those check-ins by challenging them to think of ways to improve systems. By challenging them you're now getting into innovation, which has the ability of flipping the league on its ear.

Think of the first time new schemes came into football, from the bygone days of the flying wedge to the 4-6 defense to the West Coast offense and the mobile QB. When those innovations arose the opposition was thrown into a state of disarray and the innovators ate everyone else's lunch.

So as you are advising your people on how to be even stronger performers you should also ask them to think about how things should work. What is a best case scenario? Have them answer the question "Wouldn't it be cool if..."

(That goes back to creating their Vision Statement!)

One way you can get your mature employees to become even more successful is to teach them to coach themselves. Start by having them ask themselves these questions:

- How will I know if I'm successful?
- How will I measure my progress?
- What are my priorities?
- What processes and tools did I use?
- What alternatives did I consider?
- What would I change moving forward?

A while ago, I came across one of those little question books and was really struck by the question, "Compared with 99 others your age, how successful are you?" It made me really think. First off, how do I measure/define success? Money? How happy I am? How far I've gone in my career? How short my bucket list has become?

Once I answered that for myself, I figured, "Ok, I'm doing pretty good, but there are certainly other people who are doing better, in my eyes, than I am." I decided that I was around the 75th percentile.

That in turn made me think of those people in my life who I considered to be above the 75th percentile. One of the first things I realized was that (with the possible exception of one or two very special people), there wasn't really anyone who did EVERYTHING that I considered important to be better than me.

Certainly, there were a number of guys who made more money, and a different set who seemed to have happier/better marriages, ones who were better fathers and coaches. So I looked at what were the most important pieces of life to me, made a list of them, and identified up to three people who I know just OWNED that piece in their own life. And I literally identified and wrote down each specific example of what I felt made them so good at that.

Then I called them each up and asked if I could meet with them to catch up on things. When we got together I would eventually steer the conversation to the real reason I wanted to talk, something like:

> "Jeff, you seem to do such a good job with your kids; they listen to you, they're respectful to others—it's always "please" and "thank you"...how did you and your wife pull that off??"

Or

> "You know Lauren, I'm thinking of trying to get into the Marketing department at work...I was actually a Marketing major in college and got sidetracked by the decent cash I was making as a bartender/retail manager/electrical apprentice. You're in Marketing, what would you suggest??"

Or

> "Art, I know you are a huge history buff—I was thinking of how cool it'd be to become a tour guide at the Maritime Museum; I love that place and would like to do something to get others excited about it. Do you know anyone there or have any suggestions on how to look into that??"

EVERY time I've had a conversation like this I've ALWAYS gotten a positive response and something good out of the conversation. Do you know why? It's because the one thing people like to talk the most about is—*themselves*. And it's proven that people like to be asked to give advice. If it was a good conversation that you got something out of, you should of course thank them and ask if they would mind continuing the conversation in a few weeks/months after you've had a chance to try what you discussed. I'd bet the house they'll either say yes or turn you on to someone they think might add even deeper relevance to your "research."

After that initial conversation you should (without becoming a pest) continue inviting them out for a coffee or beer just to catch up, and continue that specific conversation. Let them know what you've tried and how you've fared. They'll probably comment and add more suggestions (because again, people like to talk about themselves and their successes and like to give advice).

How often should you meet? It all depends on the size of your effort, but when I facilitate formal mentor programs I make sure the mentors and mentees meet face-to-face at least once a month for at least 45 minutes.

Gauge your situation accordingly, and remember that every conversation has a life span, meaning your initial conversation may happen in January, you get together at happy hours approximately once a month, and by April or June you may feel you have all the information you can garner from that one friend. You can still meet monthly on a friendly basis, but then it's time to move on to another person you identified and begin to do the same. And if it warrants—thank the person with a small token of appreciation, maybe a gift card to the coffee shop you've been meeting in. The power of small, personalized gifts is great and reinforces the sincerity of the relationship.

So now you have people who are running things as well as you could have ever hoped. Congratulations! What do you do next?

Leaders often mature into mentors, and the relationship looks a little different. As a leader you are guiding them, but now in your role as mentor you are really just checking in and providing insight.

It is possible that your charges have gone on to new positions (hopefully still in the company), but regardless, you want them to succeed wherever they go. So offer to be there for them. See if arranging a monthly check-in suits your schedules. It could be for an hour over a coffee or virtually, whatever it allows you the opportunity to catch up. Perhaps the discussion is entirely a social one. Perhaps it's more of them looking for thoughts on a problem they have. It could be you seeking advice from them on a problem you're facing. They are after all someone who you came to trust and respect, so what greater compliment than to ask them for their input on a problem that you have?

As they continue to develop as better leaders themselves, they will come to understand the new position you hold in their lives as a mentor and appreciate it. You could share with them how it is in everyone's best interest for them to reach back to someone and help them as well, the old Pay it Forward move. It is an incredibly rewarding relationship, another win-win! Damn, with all these wins you might as well just hoist that Super Bowl trophy right now!

The amount of time you interact with these folks is going to become less and less. That's good, because you may still have some rookies on your team who need a little more attention as we've covered in the earlier chapters. It will also give you time to focus on higher-level strategic items that you should be focusing on.

You can still do your weekly check-ins with them, but they aren't going to last nearly as long. You can spend a little bit of time with them just to catch up on other personal issues, which just strengthens the relationship.

I hope you can see how this is truly a win-win situation as everyone grows! It all gets back to the adage of growing the pie. You shouldn't think, "How can I get a bigger slice of the pie so that people around me get smaller slices?", but instead you should think, "How exactly do we grow the pie?" And this is it!

Obviously if employees are still coming to you with questions about how to handle more basic items, they aren't ready for this stage yet. But for those who are, you just tell them, "You do what you think is best" when they have a problem and assure them that they've got this!

As I mentioned before, the sexiest thing in the world is confidence. Everybody loves a confident person as long as they are not cocky. People follow confident people.

Tell your team players outright, "For the next year we are working on your confidence. I want you to make decisions with the confidence that you are making the right ones." Let them know that you don't expect 100% of the time for them to perfectly nail their decisions, because that is impossible.

Think about it. Your decisions are not always perfect, correct? You should much rather want to have a person make a decision that is 60% or 80% right than a person who makes no decision at all. Better done than waiting for perfection.

Coaches make imperfect decisions, QBs make imperfect decisions. But skilled, trained, confident coaches and players who share the vision, given leeway to call it as they see it, produce victories for the team.

Go to the Replay Booth

1. Intentionally developing intrapreneurship increases innovation
2. Formal in-house mentoring programs are highly beneficial
3. Confidence is key to success!

Reviewing LEAD

So with the extra time you'll have NOT managing your people, you can now spend the majority of your time on strategic planning, revisiting the SWOT for the next job to tackle, and setting up appointments with those who can help you achieve your mid-term and long-term goals as well as new targets. The value is you have time to be more strategic and not just tactical with the day-to-day.

Plan with other managers in your organization to tackle items off of your SWOT analysis and goals and revisit your goals from last year. Are those accomplishments still holding strong or need to be addressed? If they need to be addressed, is someone on your team ready for a new project?? That can be part of their new growth plan/goal for the upcoming fiscal year!

LOCKER ROOM AFTER THE BIG WIN

Congratulations team, you did it! You plowed through this book like an unstoppable machine! You reflected on theory, laughed at the lighter side of professional life, and gained understanding of how to better lead the business you control. You've relived some great football moments, relived some movie quotes, and hopefully learned a few new things from our contributors.

Game ball: You!

Hopefully you've gotten some new ideas on how to lead your team, or at minimum, refreshed what you knew but had maybe forgotten. The goal of *Down Set Lead* is to give you an improved or refreshed idea of how to tackle the ins and outs of everyday business, get altitude above the line of scrimmage so you can see the whole field, and scheme a winning plan that makes all the players on the field feel proud of who they are and what they do to get the win.

If there's one last movie quote I can leave you with, it's this:

> *"You're playing small doesn't serve the world. We were born to make manifest the glory of God that is within us. It's not just in some of us; it's in everyone. And as we let our own light shine, we unconsciously give other people permission to do the same. As we are liberated from our own fear, our presence automatically liberates others."*
>
> — RICK GONZALEZ AS TIMO CRUZ IN
> *COACH CARTER* (2005)

Just remember that the vast majority of people want to be led. The vast majority of people will follow an ethical, average leader without much grumbling. The opportunity for you to grow as a leader and help others grow, is there every day. Just like a football coach makes his or her game plan, you can make yours to be a better leader, create a stronger team that isn't afraid to be innovative, learn from calculated risks, and welcome the wins that come from their work.

Once the workflow gets nailed down and the players begin to effectively execute their job duties, you can begin to strategically plan beyond the next cycle, week, or month and begin to target long-term sustainable growth and succession. You can become more proactive in your community and begin to create a dynasty that ties your name to the good that is happening inside and outside your building.

Look into your teammates' eyes, tell them your vision, how they play into making that success happen, and listen to their words. Stay calm, remind them that whatever happens that the sun will rise again in the east tomorrow, and that by acting together you'll get down the field, communicating at the huddle, audibling as necessary to work your way down field, overcoming obstacles, and scoring before the clock hits 0:00. And when the dust settles, you will then have your dynasty.

CONNECT WITH OUR CONTRIBUTORS!

I would like to personally thank all the men who shared their personal reflections throughout the book. They've gone from being football personnel into transformative leaders. Read more about them and how to connect with them in the following pages.

JEDIDIAH COLLINS / *OWN*

Jedidiah was a two-sport letterman (football and basketball) at Mission Viejo High School (CA). At Washington State he set a school record in 2007 for most catches by a tight end. He was drafted into the NFL, and went from being cut 12 times to being the #1 Fullback in the NFL and earn accolades as a New Orleans Saint.

Jedidiah is the Founder and CEO of Money Vehicle, a 10 module curriculum designed to entertain and engage students through their financial journey. Its Mission is to empower students and young professionals to U.S.E. money (Understand, Strategize, Efficient) and begin a financial plan.

Jedidiah has a big heart, beautiful vision for kids and is great to chat with.

Connect with Jedidiah at jed@yourmoneyvehicle.com

Visit the Your Money Vehicle website here

JEFF DIAMOND / *NEGOTIATE*

Jeff Diamond is a retired NFL executive. He worked for the Minnesota Vikings from 1976 to 1998, during which time he rose from a minor post in public relations to the position of Senior Vice President and General Manager.

In 1999, after being named NFL Executive of the Year, he was hired away by the Tennessee Titans to be President of that organization, and remained in that post until his retirement in 2004.

During his time as an NFL executive, Diamond's teams went to the Super Bowl once (the Titans after the 1999 season). While Senior Vice President for the Vikings, the team achieved a franchise high of 15 wins during the 1998 regular season

Jeff does corporate and college speaking (to MBA, Law School and under-grad classes/symposiums) on the subjects of Negotiation, Labor Relations, Leadership, Strategic Management, Team Building and Sports Business/ Sports Management.

Jeff is incredibly bright and full of interesting insights.

If you are interested in having him speak to your group, class, or symposium, contact him at: diamondj4@comcast.net

MARQUES OGDEN / *LISTEN*

Marques played offensive tackle and center with the Jacksonville Jaguars, Baltimore Ravens, Buffalo Bills, and Tennessee Titans. He is now a keynote speaker, business coach, and corporate consultant with a unique approach to elevating your success to the next level. Marques creates presentations designed to help each brand in various elements of business - communication, sales, leadership, management, generational issues, transition, innovation, customer experience, diversity and inclusion, and more. His presentations are customized to a more traditional approach designed around The Success Cycle, which brings value back to the core basics of fundamental relationship building and success.

Marques has an infectious personality and a wonderful flow to his talks.

Connect with Marques at www.marquesogden.com

DOUG PLANK / *EMPOWER*

Doug played safety for the Chicago Bears under Buddy Ryan, and was the first Bears rookie ever to lead the team in tackles. Plank wore number 46, and it was from his style of play that Ryan gave the name for the 4-6 defense he created that eventually became renowned for its incredible effectiveness against offensive schemes of the era. San Francisco 49er's Hall Of Fame coach Bill Walsh said this about it: "I had to use every bit of knowledge and experience and wisdom I had to come up with game plans to attack this defense. It's really the most singular innovation in defensive football in the last twenty years."

Doug now works as a motivational speaker, business consultant and sports analyst for Sports USA Media, covering NFL and NCAA football for national radio and online broadcasts including the Armed Forces Network.

Doug's huge heart comes out immediately as he talks. His stories are full of passion.

Connect with Doug via email: dougplank46@gmail.com

APPENDIX

What Employees Want

Well over a decade ago a now-famous study gave what was then considered surprising insight on what employees wanted from their bosses and companies:

1. Interesting work
2. Full appreciation for work done
3. Feeling of being in on things
4. Job security
5. Good pay
6. Promotion and growth
7. Good working conditions
8. Loyalty to employees
9. Tactful discipline
10. Help with personal problems

While a lot has changed since then, I could argue that a lot of those points at/towards the top are still very relevant. That said, here's what a more recent study (2013 *Inc. Magazine*) found:

1. To feel proud
2. To be treated fairly
3. To respect the boss
4. To be heard out
5. To have a personal life
6. To be coached not micromanaged
7. To see the assholes get fired
8. To feel less stress
9. To have a little security
10. To beat the competition

And now, after the COVID pandemic and stepping through the Great Resignation and Quiet Quitting we have something like this (2022 CNN Business Poll):

1. Compensation
2. Work-life balance
3. Chance to play to their strengths
4. Job security
5. Vaccination policies that align with job seekers' beliefs
6. Diversity and inclusiveness

Why the changes?

We've gone from a Baby Boomer dominated workforce to one with Gen Xers, Millennials (the largest generation by far now in the workforce) and the incoming Gen Z's. The last two have especially had much different experiences growing up from the Boomer's experiences and attitudes, and the world is a different place with different technologies and priorities.

It's important to realize these are not identical surveys, so while the outcomes are fairly different, there are some key underlying similarities, essentially respect, fairness and opportunity.

NEW LEADER ONBOARDING SESSION

One way to help establish trust from the outset is by conducting a New Leader Onboarding Session. This exercise will help increase trust by breaking down communication barriers.

The New Leader Onboarding Session works best when a new boss comes on board, but holding such a session will still be beneficial for a boss who's been around for a while, especially if they suspect that there is a legitimate lack of trust.

- Select an outsider to facilitate

- Before the meeting, have the new incoming employee/manager list what they want others to know about her or him. Post this on the wall, covered up at the beginning

- Pull the team together in one room, have them each list what they want to share with the new person, and post this on the wall

- Have team members list the questions they want to ask of the new manager and post this on the wall

- Bring the newly hired employee/manager in to read and address the lists on the wall aloud and then show and give their information that was covered on the wall.

When everything from the sheets on the wall is covered, the facilitator should ask if there's anything else anyone would like to add or ask for clarity. If time and budget allow, having a short social with a small snack would be a great touch; that would allow for informal conversation to start and the connections to grow in a safe environment.

While this won't instantly create trust, it is very powerful and will certainly help institute a more fertile opportunity for success more quickly.

ACKNOWLEDGEMENTS

Lots of people helped me in putting this book together, and they deserve my thanks, most notably:

My editor, chief cheerleader, and guide Lee Crumbaugh. This project would not have come to fruition without him.

My accountability partners who kept me on task, especially Rob; but also Becca, Dan, Gigi, and "Skinny" Rod.

Proofreaders Joy, Mike, Pat Mac and Ted really kicked (my) butt on this project. Thanks!!

Kim, Jay, Jesse, Renee, Emily, Mel, Trigg, Tyler, Donovan, Zach, Tom, Helen—thank you very much for your support and input!

I have great appreciation for these folks and lots of others who cheered me on to this accomplishment—thank you everybody!!

GLOSSARY OF TERMS USED IN THIS BOOK

DiSC: DiSC® assessments are behavioral self-assessment tools based on the emotional and behavioral theory of psychologist William Marston. The tool is designed to predict job performance, the theory describing personality through four central traits: dominance, inducement, submission, and compliance.

EBITDA: stands for earnings before interest, taxes, depreciation, and amortization, a key performance measure of corporate profitability.

Johari Window: is a mapping technique designed to help people better understand their relationship with themselves and others. It uses four quadrants to identify what is Open to all, a Façade set for others, Hidden to our own selves, or Unknown to everyone.

MBTI: The Myers-Briggs Type Indicator® assessment; in personality typology, it is an introspective self-report questionnaire indicating differing psychological preferences in how people perceive the world and make decisions. The test attempts to assign four categories: introversion or extraversion, sensing or intuition, thinking or feeling, and judging or perceiving.

Pay it Forward: The concept that when someone does something for you, instead of paying that person back directly, you pass it on to another person instead. (In the opinion of the author, the movie of the same title, while about the same concept, was just plain horrible.)

SWOT: SWOT (strengths, weaknesses, opportunities, and threats) analysis is a framework used to evaluate a company's competitive position and to develop strategic planning

ENDNOTES

1   http://athlonsports.com/college-football/athlon-archive-peyton-manning-takes-reigns-tennessee#sthash.X6zqRbcw.dpuf

2   https://www.nbrii.com/employee-survey-white-papers/engaged-or-disengaged-that-is-the-question/

3   I would strongly recommend waiting until at least your second interview to ask these deeper questions about the specifics regarding who is on staff.

ABOUT THE AUTHOR

With a passion to improve people and organizations, Rod has held a variety of leadership roles with stints in human resources, training and organizational development, nonprofit development, and leadership programming.

In the community Rod serves as a mentor and coach; he founded two Baltimore area programs: Anna's Guys, a collection of men who work with abused and sheltered children; and the Catch A Pig 5k, having raising nearly $100k for the local Boys & Girls Clubs.

He earned his Bachelor's degree in Business Administration at Towson University, and a Masters of Organizational Development from Johns Hopkins University.

Look for my next book!

Already in the works: Everything I Needed to Know I Learned Watching Bill Murray Movies ...or something titled along those lines.

I'm tying key life lessons to a number of Bill Murray movies, from *Meatballs* on. I hope you get a chance to read that one too!

Connect with me on LinkedIn!	Check out my Tik Tok videos!

It's my go-to social media site!   Lots of great/fun content here!

ABOUT DOWN SET LEAD

Down Set Lead is a group of dedicated professionals who assist in growing you, your people, and your future.

Our passion is making people and organizations better through strategic growth initiatives, training, and coaching. We believe in using the power of diversity, mentoring, vision and creativity to achieve a greater good.

We excel in designing and delivering experiential learning programs, such as:

- Leadership in the Battlefield: one- and two-day trips to regional battlefields to learn how decisions from a 18th or 19th century battle relates to making good business decisions today.

- The Amazing Challenge: Based off the show *The Amazing Race*, a team building program that ties classroom learning with completing team challenges in your local neighborhood involving other local businesses.

- In-house Mentoring: a program that ties HIPEs (HIgh Potential Employees) with seasoned leaders at your organization, exponentially growing everyone's skills and knowledge while also increasing your productivity and retention rates.

- Down Set Start: group coaching for young professionals.

As well as Keynoting and Coaching (one-on-one and team based opportunities for employees at all levels).

Connect with us here! https://downsetlead.com/